HEROES

from the

WALL

HEROES

from the

WALL

JOHN DOUGLAS FOSTER

To order additional copies of this book, contact:
Xlibris Corporation
1-888-795-4274
www.Xlibris.com
Orders@Xlibris.com
109756

When the author John Douglas Foster was wounded while serving in Vietnam during Tet '68, he received more than a piece of metal in his body; haunting memories of comrades opened his soul in a quest to learn more about those who didn't return. Far more important than mere names on a monument are the lives of those who died. Memorials to those who die in war need to confront us with real, living persons, with dreams and plans, hobbies and interests, connections to others, who might say something or do something that lingers forever in our heart and soul.

Foster's book provides an opportunity to grasp truly great individuals, not just numbers and statistics, not just names. For those

Who fight the battles, their fallen brothers and sisters forever live in them. This book helps ensure that they will never be forgotten by future generations who didn't know them on the battlefield. Their quirks of personality, playful antics, heroic actions, compassion and care for others, their caring and sharing with their comrades, tender concern for their family, affirmation of life while engulfed in places of death, and so much more, captivate our attention. Though dead, they vividly live.

It is common for those who fight in war to say that they were never closer to another person than those with whom they fought, and that in combat they lived with the best men, as a group, they ever have known. We, too, are privileged to meet some of these through this book.

We learn of their roots in places like the war-ravaged lands of Finland, the poverty of a large family in New York. We learn how they fell in love and married, just before going to war and dying. We hear of their premonitions of dying. We learn of heroism that contains great fears, like the greater sky shadowed with dark clouds. We read deeply moving and perspective words by a Sergeant written of his Lieutenant. We learn of a grown woman who learns of a father killed in Vietnam—eventually verifying this through DNA and subsequently brought into a large caring family who related to her a father she never knew, his passion for music and making people laugh. We learn of a nurse, one of eight on the Vietnam Memorial Wall. We learn of a Chaplain whose love for the Marines he served moved him to lay down his life for them. We learn of a POW's captivity and ordeal. We learn so much more, and the war becomes more than statistics, tactics, results of winning or losing, but becomes a tapestry woven with individual threads of its participants. We learn of the true cost of war and we learn of the true humanity hidden beneath all the mud, gore, hardness, and ugliness we confront in war.

Mr. Foster's book not only gives us a monument of lives; he provides us with a legacy for future generations to grasp with a better understanding of the Vietnam War.

—**Rev. Ray W. Stubbe**
US Navy Chaplain,
Siege at Khe Sanh, 1968

An unknown name on a gravestone is as dead as the person in the grave—until someone tells you a story about that person. John Foster, in Heroes From the Wall, has brought dead names on the Vietnam memorial Wall to life through telling the stories behind the names. With careful research, interviews with people who knew the men, and a story-teller's eye for the detail that captures the character of the person behind the name, Foster reveals the heart, hopes, dreams and ultimate sacrifices that were made by these soldiers and Marines. A Vietnam veteran himself, the author's respect for his subjects is communicated loud and clear. The reader is given a portal through the smooth reflections on the smooth granite into the real lives, the real people, who died so young. These unsung heroes have now been sung.

—**Karl Marlantes**
author of New York Times best seller
Matterhorn

"Whether one served in Vietnam or not, HEROES FROM THE WALL cannot be read without shedding a tear. For those who did serve there, who experienced the bond formed by those serving together in combat and who suffered a loss from among a cherished band of brothers, this book reinforces that which we knew - the bond is never broken. As the stories are told of those lost on Vietnam's battlefields, only a few from among the 58,195 stories on the Vietnam Veteran's Memorial Wall, we once again experience the pain of their loss but, decades later, can also join in celebration of their lives as heroes. It is important for young people to read about the life stories of an earlier generation's young men who answered America's call to fight an unpopular war, selflessly giving of themselves. Our fallen brothers cannot be forgotten. "HEROES FROM THE WALL" makes sure the reader will not.

> —Lt. Col James G. Zumwalt,
> USMC (Ret)
> Author of "Bare Feet, Iron Will—
> Stories From the Other Side of
> Vietnam's Battlefields"

Of the more than 58,000 killed in Vietnam, not much of a personal nature of these brave patriots is known. Heroes From the Wall *addresses this omission, and I recommend it to historians and to freedom loving Americans. The selfless devotion to country by our heroes should be recognized and applauded by all!*

> —Wulf R. Lindenau
> Commander General
> Military Order of Foreign Wars of the US

Heroes From the Wall *is an important piece of work. I am drawn by the stories of these unsung heroes of the Vietnam War. Anyone who reads this book will also be drawn and they will realize the value of freedom for which they are now enjoying.*

> —Colonel Richard Rosser
> US Marine Corps (Ret.)
> Vietnam 1967-1968

This book is dedicated to my loving and lovely wife, Noelly Gold-Foster. Without her support, this book may have never been completed. If I were to tell Noelly that I am going to dig a hole to China, she would be behind me all the way, often with a shovel to backfill the hole as I dig. Nevertheless, she has my back, and I am thankful for that.

AUTHOR'S NOTE

The information in this book is based on interviews of family and friends of the fallen. Other sources include the Virtual Wall website, newspaper articles, *Leatherneck* magazine, *Vietnam* magazine, after-action reports, and various military documents. Also, books, witness interviews, and other authorities. In some cases, due to lapse of time and participants not remembering exact details of certain situations, dialogue and paraphrasing were inserted to match the situation. I would like to thank all those people and their sources for making this book possible.

CONTENTS

PREFACE

Vietnam was my war. Its effect on me was personal. The political agenda meant nothing to me. Survival meant everything to me. As a nineteen-year-old lance corporal with Echo Company, Second Battalion, Ninth Marines, survival in the Northern I Corps was a 24-7 job. I saw many Marines maimed for life, and I saw many Marines die. Many of these Marines, like me, were only nineteen years old, yet they were men matured beyond their years.

While going on patrols, I personally insisted on walking point. I only trusted my instincts. I did not want another Marine to walk us into an ambush. On February 2, 1968, while engaged in a firefight on Hill 37 near Cam Lo, I took a hit with an AK-47. The bullet entered the right side of my cartridge belt and exited the left side of the belt. Doctors at First Medical Battalion in Da Nang told me that the bullet missed my spine by one-eighth of a centimeter. I survived the ordeal despite the fact that I led my squad into an ambush.

I believe that while in Vietnam, my attitude was cold and callous. "Better them than me."

In 1998, I made my first visit to the Vietnam Memorial Wall. It was during Veterans Day. I was in awe of the thousands of visitors. The flowers, wreaths, combat boots, photos, and even a six-pack of beer were among many items laid at the base of the Wall. I felt like I was in a trance. Everyone was moving in slow motion. A man with a gray beard was atop a ladder rubbing a name. There were tears in his eyes. I believe that there were tears in almost everyone's eyes that day. I had remembered a Marine that I served with in the States. We trained together, and we were on the same flight to Vietnam. I turned to look at the Wall, and there was his name: GARY D. KELLER. It was like he was calling me. A lady with the Park Service patted me on the back. As I turned to acknowledge her, she handed me a tissue. I thanked her and told her that to many of the tourists visiting, these are just names on a wall. She agreed, and then she explained that most visitors were Vietnam veterans like myself; and that many of them, like myself, had friends that died in Vietnam. She also told me that thousands of these names have been memorialized on the Virtual Wall website.

When I returned home from Washington, DC, I logged on to the Virtual Wall site to post memorials for two of my stateside buddies that died in Vietnam: Gary Keller and Michael Zuniga. While on the site, I viewed a few memorials. I was in awe. The men I was reading about were real and honorable heroes. One such man happened to be my platoon commander while in Vietnam, First Lieutenant John Carson. I had recently learned that he was killed a few months after I was medically evacuated. I read randomly about Army Master Sergeant Gabriel Alamo's memorial and was touched, not only by his service to his country but by his love for his family.

I asked myself, "Why is it just me and a few veterans that are reading these memorials?" It was then that I realized that I wanted to share the stories of these heroes with today's younger generation. I wrote a letter to Deborah Alamo and asked her permission to further honor her father in my book. I also told her that I was not out to make a profit on this book. If I am fortunate to get it published, all profits will be donated to the Vietnam Veteran's Memorial Fund and the Make-a-Wish Foundation. This was her response:

Thank you so much for your kind letter. And I would like to thank you also for accepting the call to defend our country.

Of course you have my permission to write about my dad. I believe that our young people need more positive role models today. Someone other than the musicians and athletes that they emulate so much, and then see them on the 6 o'clock news being hauled into court on charges for drugs, alcohol or sexual abuse. If your book gets into the hands of just one teenager and inspires him or her to do something positive with their life, then your effort will have rewards worth far more than money. What we are is God's gift to us. What we become is our gift to God.

Sincerely,
Deb

I have requested permission from family and friends of all the men I have written about in this book. I have been overwhelmed by their support and enthusiasm. God bless every one of them. And this is for all the men and women that have made the ultimate sacrifice for our freedom and may they rest in peace.

THE MEMORIAL

One of the unfortunate legacies of the Vietnam War is that the United States virtually turned its back on those who fought in its most controversial overseas conflict. The old-line veterans' service organizations, for example, all but shunned Vietnam War returnees. The Veterans Administration all but ignored Vietnam veterans seeking compensation for diseases caused by exposure to Agent Orange and those asking for mental therapy as a result of their traumatic war experiences. Too many in the antiwar movement blamed the warriors for the war. And Congress did nothing at all for Vietnam veterans until the early 1980s and 1990s.

The corollary to that situation is that the men and women who had served in the Vietnam War had to lead the fight for just about every government program and every other sort of recognition of their service to America themselves. That includes conceiving of, lobbying Congress for, and raising funds to build the Vietnam Veterans Memorial in Washington, DC, an edifice that has become one of the nation's most revered works of architecture since it was dedicated nearly thirty years ago.

When Jan Scruggs, a former 199th Light Infantry Brigade soldier, went to see the Vietnam War movie *The Deer Hunter* in 1979, he came out of the theater with an audacious plan: build a national memorial on the Mall in Washington listing the names of those who had perished in the war. Scruggs, who had come home from Vietnam with eleven pieces of shrapnel in his body, was working for the federal government at the time. In his spare time, Scruggs organized the Vietnam Veteran's Memorial Fund (VVMF)—with fellow Vietnam veterans Robert Doubek, Robert Kimmett, and John Wheeler—to attempt to turn his vision into a reality.

The Memorial Fund wanted Vietnam veterans to have a tangible symbol of recognition from the American people. By separating the issue of the service of the individual men and women from the issue of US policy in Vietnam, the Memorial Fund hoped to begin a process of national reconciliation.

Initial support came from US Senators Charles Mathias Jr. (R-MD) and John W. Warner (R-VA). On November 8, 1979, Senator Mathias introduced legislation to authorize a site of national park land for the memorial. The first significant financial contributions to launch the fundraising campaign were raised by Senator Warner.

More than $8,000,000 was raised, all from private sources. More than 275,000 Americans donated the majority of the money needed to build the memorial.

On July 1, 1980, Congress authorized a site of three acres in Constitutional Gardens near the Lincoln Memorial. In October that year, VVMF announced a national design competition. Within a couple of months, there were over 2,500 registrants. The competition was the largest ever held in the United States. About 1,421 design entries were submitted. All entries were judged anonymously by a jury of eight internationally recognized artists and designers who had been selected by the VVMF. On May 1, 1981, the jury presented its unanimous selection for first prize, which was accepted and adopted enthusiastically by the Memorial Fund. The winning design was the work of Maya Ying Lin, of Athens, Ohio, a twenty-one-year-old senior at Yale University. In August 1981, the VVMF selected a building company and architecture firm to develop the plans and build Lin's design. Maya Lin was the design consultant for the architect of record.

A statement by Maya Lin, which was part of her competition submission in March 1981:

Walking through this park-like area, the memorial appears as a rift in the earth, a long, polished, black stone wall, emerging from and receding into the earth. Approaching the memorial, the ground slopes gently downward and the low walls emerging on either side, growing out of the earth, extend and converge at a point below and ahead. Walking into this grassy site contained by the walls of the memorial we can barely make out the carved names upon the memorial's walls. These names seemingly infinite in number, convey the sense of overwhelming numbers, while unifying these individuals into a whole.

The memorial is composed not as an unchanging monument, but as a moving composition to be understood as we move into and out of it. The passage itself is gradual; the descent to the origin slow, but it is at the origin that the memorial is to be fully understood. At the intersection of these walls, on the right side, is carved the date of the first death. It is followed by the names of those who died in the war, in chronological order. These names continue on this wall appearing to recede into the earth at the wall's end. The names resume on the left wall as the wall emerges from the earth, continuing back to the origin where the date of the last death is carved at the bottom of this wall. Thus the war's beginning and end meet; the war is 'complete,' coming full-circle, yet broken by the earth that bounds the angle's open side, and continued within the earth itself. As we turn to leave, we see these walls stretching into the distance, directing us to the Washington Monument, to the left, and the Lincoln Memorial, to the right, thus bringing the Vietnam Memorial into a historical context. We the living are brought to a concrete realization of these deaths. Brought to a sharp awareness of such a loss, it is up to each individual to resolve or come to terms with this loss. For death, is in the end a personal and private matter, and the area contained with this memorial is a quiet place, meant for personal reflection and private reckoning. The black granite walls, each two hundred feet long, and ten feet below ground at their lowest point (gradually ascending toward ground level) effectively act as sound barrier, yet are of such a height and length so as not to appear threatening or enclosing. The actual area is wide and shallow, allowing for a sense of privacy, and the sunlight from the memorial's southern exposure along with the grassy park surrounding and within its walls, contribute to the serenity of the area. Thus this memorial is for those who have died, and for us to remember them. The memorial's origin is located approximately at the center of the site; its legs each extending two hundred feet towards the Washington Monument and the Lincoln Memorial. The walls, contained on one side by the earth, are ten feet below ground at their point of origin, gradually lessening in height, until they finally recede totally into the earth, at their ends. The walls are to be made of a hard, polished black granite, with the names to be carved in a simple Trojan letter. The memorial's construction involves re-contouring the area within the wall's boundaries, so as to provide for an easily accessible descent, but as much of the site as possible should be left untouched. The area should remain as a park, for all to enjoy.

Each wall is 248 feet, 8 inches, forming a 125-degree 12-minute angle, 10 feet 1.5 inches tall at their vertex.

Maya Lin

GARY DALE KELLER

    Had it not been for Gary Keller, this book would have never been written. After posting his memorial on the Virtual Wall website, I began to view other memorials on the site. I was overwhelmed by the character of those men that sacrificed their lives for their fellow comrades. I was equally overwhelmed by the positive responses that I received from family and friends that allowed me to further honor these men in this book.

I first met Gary Keller during advanced infantry training at Camp Pendleton, California, in late 1966. All the Marines looked alike in their olive drab utilities (fatigues) and with their very short-cropped haircuts.

One stood out from the others. He appeared to be more mature. With no black insignia chevrons visible on his collars, I thought, perhaps he is an officer. He was a private.

It was our first day at the training facility, and we were being assigned billeting in Quonset huts. As I was putting my gear away near my bunk, a Marine tapped me on the shoulder. "My name is Gary Keller, and I am from Yakima, Washington." I introduced myself as Private First Class John Foster. I was surprised that Gary had just completed boot camp. I thought he was older, but he was just eighteen years old, the same as me.

After we got settled into our new quarters, all the troops got called out onto the parade deck for a promotion ceremony. There were about six Marines getting promoted. Most of them were privates first class being promoted to lance corporals. Gary was one of them. He was getting his first promotion to private first class (PFC).

After the ceremony, we were given weekend liberty. Gary and I walked over to the base exchange. He wanted to buy new PFC chevrons for his uniforms, and I wanted to call home. While I was talking to my Mom at the pay phone, I spotted Gary walking by with captain's bars on his collar. I couldn't believe what I was seeing. Other Marines were rendering the respectful salute as they passed Captain Keller. One of them was a lieutenant. I immediately hung up the phone and made my way toward Gary. As I approached him, I saluted the captain so as not to arouse any suspicion. I pulled him aside. "What in the hell are you doing? Do you want to get court-martialed?" He told me that he just wanted to see what it was like to be saluted on. I took off the captain's bars and put on his new PFC chevrons.

Gary and I became very good friends. We spent most of our off-duty hours together. One weekend we had a three-day pass and decided to hitchhike to my hometown of Santa Cruz, California. We caught a ride immediately. Gary introduced himself to the driver in his usual manner. "My name is Gary Keller, and I'm from Yakima." The driver, who was traveling to San Francisco, gave us a ride all the way to Santa Cruz, which was a seven-hour drive. Gary kept the driver and I entertained for the whole trip with his stories of life in Yakima.

When the driver dropped us off at my mom's house, Gary gave the driver a $100 bill. In the Marine Corps, that was more than what a private made in a month. That $100 could have paid for both of us to fly round-trip. Perhaps Gary was a wealthy man, or maybe he was just generous. I prefer to think the latter.

After four weeks of intense infantry training, we were ready to take on the Viet Cong and the entire North Vietnamese Army. Gary wasn't scared at all.

He told me that he was looking forward to visiting a lush tropical country and meeting some of the locals.

Our flight to Vietnam was aboard a Flying Tiger 727 from Norton Air Force Base in Riverside, California. Gary began introducing himself to the flight attendants and crew. "My name is Gary Keller, and I'm from Yakima."

We were a bunch of eighteen- and nineteen-year-olds on our way to war, yet Gary helped make the flight reasonably pleasant. He returned all the money he won in poker games. "Can't spend it where I'm going" was his reasoning. And if he saw a Marine who seemed nervous or scared, Gary would sit with him and strike up a conversation that inevitably put the young Marine at ease.

As we disembarked the plane in Da Nang, the young Marines were pleading for a "last good-bye kiss" from the flight attendants. They obliged with only a hug. As Gary was leaving the plane, he said good-bye to one of the ladies and then whispered something in her ear. She replied with a kiss on the lips. He never revealed to me what he had whispered. Must have been his charm.

There was a staging area in Da Nang for all the new arrivals. Unlike the war in Iraq, we never deployed as a unit. We went over as a group, and when we got to the staging area, we were assigned to units. I was immediately assigned to Echo Company, Second Battalion, Ninth Marines, Third Marine Division, which was headquartered at Camp Carroll near the DMZ. I was put on a chopper and headed north to my new home before Gary was assigned his unit.

It was 1967, and some of the fiercest fighting of the Vietnam War was taking place. During this intense fighting, along with the Ninth Marines, I only thought of survival. Sometimes during quiet time, I wondered how Gary was doing. I wondered which infantry unit he was assigned. I thought of him often. I knew that he would use his charm to help him survive. Gary was a machine-gunner, and he was good at his job. But somehow I envisioned him in the rear with the gear and making life comfortable for himself and other Marines.

I was wounded during the Tet Offensive of 1968. My wound was not life threatening but serious enough to get me medically evacuated back to the United States.

While recuperating in Tripler Army Hospital in Hawaii, someone had given me a May 1968 issue of *Leatherneck*, the magazine for Marines. In that issue was an article about the Battle of Hue. And there was a picture of Lance Corporal Gary Keller providing cover for his men with his M-60 machine gun. He was with Hotel Company, Second Battalion, Fifth Marines, First Marine Division. That short caption under his picture was all I needed for a mailing address.

When I got home, I wrote Gary a letter, and in it was a picture of me, my girlfriend, and my 1956 Chevy. I was teasing Gary and telling him, "Haha! I made it home before you did." I never did get a letter back.

Approximately a year later, while attending Marine Security Guard School at Henderson Hall, Arlington, Virginia, I ran into an MP (military police) who also trained with Gary and myself. He was on the flight that took us to Vietnam. His name was Rooker. He was also with Hotel 2/5. He told me that Gary had shown him the letter that I sent. "Well, the dirty rat didn't write back," I said. Rooker told me that Gary had been killed in July 1968. I was devastated. I was in a state of total shock. I wanted to call someone. I wanted to call Gary's family but didn't know their names or whom to contact.

I still have that issue of *Leatherneck*. I often look at it, particularly on Memorial Day and Veterans Day.

I have attempted calls to numerous Kellers listed in the Yakima white pages with no luck. I thought that by posting a memorial on the Virtual Wall website, I might flush out a family member.

The week before Veterans Day 2008, I finally got smart. Forty years after Gary's death, I made contact with the *Yakima Herald-Republic* newspaper and talked to one of their editors, Barbara Serrano. I asked if I could publish a story about one of Yakima's fallen on Veterans Day. "Of course, we would be honored," was her response.

The story was published on Veterans Day and was well appreciated by the people of Yakima. One praise printed in the Letters to the Editor section reads:

> *My wife and I just wanted to say thank you for the Veterans Day guest commentary, "A friend never forgotten."*
>
> *We read the story to our family on Veterans Day morning. I thank John Foster, the guest commentator, for sharing his experience with Gary Keller from Yakima as they went through basic training as young Marines and then headed off to Vietnam, where Gary gave his life for his country.*
>
> *John's words about Gary's charm, and the kind of man that he was, who cared about others and went out of his way to make them feel better, deeply touched our family. I wish Gary had made it back, and I somehow could have known him. We are so thankful that he, and so many other great men and women like him, have been willing not only to comfort their friends and others in difficult times, but to pay the ultimate price for all of our freedom. Veterans are the life blood of democracy, and without them, it surely would die.*
>
> *Thank you John Foster and thank you Gary Keller.*
>
> Shon Copeland, Yakima, Washington

I hoped a family member of Gary's would see the article and call me. Sure enough, they did.

At 10:00 a.m. the day the article was published, I received a call from Lynn Keller Locke. Lynn is Gary's sister, and she still lives in Yakima. I had a lump in my throat the size of a golf ball. I didn't quite know what to say. I didn't have to say anything. She was so grateful, and she expressed her gratitude with tears of joy and sadness at the same time.

She said, "I was woken out of bed. My aunt called and actually got me and Mom out of bed. We couldn't believe what she was telling us ... We said, 'Who is this guy? I don't remember Gary mentioning a John Foster. Do you?'"

Lynn told me she is still living with her ninety-year-old mother, Anna, in the same house where she, Gary, and a younger brother, Dave, were raised. She was two years older than Gary.

I was so overwhelmed with the conversation. It was kind of surreal. There were even a couple of times when there was dead silence.

She told me the family had been struggling after her parents divorced. Gary found them all a job in a warehouse and apparently got some of his friends jobs there too. These kids were working, and his sister worked there. His mother worked there too. The workers thought that all of them were Anna's kids because they all called her mom.

Gary Keller was not your typical Marine. He did not have that hard-charging, gung-ho attitude. He was too laid-back. His appearance was not important to him, and because of that, he did not do well when it came to inspections. Gary was more concerned for "the other guy." With that in mind, I asked Lynn why Gary joined the Marine Corps.

She told me that when Gary was a teenager, he had gotten into a little bit of trouble. He and some friends had been stealing things from homes, and they got caught. The judge had told Gary he had two choices: join the military or go to jail. Gary chose the Marine Corps.

Lynn then handed the telephone to her mother. I now have two golf-ball-sized lumps in my throat. There was more gratitude and more tears. Anna was mostly apologizing for crying. I said, "You know, that's perfectly okay. If it makes you feel any better, I'm crying too." "Bless your heart," she told me. "You've been a godsend. We're just so thrilled that you remembered my son."

The following day, I received a call from Ida Mullinax of Graham, Washington. Ida is Gary's aunt, and she was the first to read the article on Veterans Day. One of Ida's stories about Gary was how he used to love riding motorcycles. He liked to go fast, and he rarely wore a helmet.

She remembered one time when Gary rode over Chinook Pass to their house near Burien. He came rolling into the driveway on his bike with his face covered in bugs. That I would love to have seen.

Gary has several cousins in that area, and one of them, Don Mullinax, also served in Vietnam. He had done construction work near the DMZ with the Sea Bees. He had already spent two tours in Vietnam and was stationed in Japan when Gary was killed. Anna had requested that Don escort Gary's body home.

One of the reasons I had written the article in the *Yakima Herald* was to let the people of Yakima know a local hero will not be forgotten. Gary was never awarded any medals for valor, but he was a hero just the same. Gary was proficient as a machine-gunner, and it was that proficiency that allowed many of his fellow Marines to come home. That in itself carries a lot of status among the men in a combat unit.

I was very excited about having my article published in the *Yakima Herald-Republic*. In fact, I was so excited that I sent the article to *Sgt Grit*. *Sgt Grit* is a weekly newsletter exclusively for Marines and Marine families. Just as the *Yakima Herald* brought me Gary's family, *Sgt Grit* brought me some of the men that served with Gary in Vietnam.

Gary Dale Keller's name is located on the Vietnam Memorial Wall, panel 50W, line 39.

Juan Luis Terrazas

One Sunday morning in the fall of 2005, while having my morning cup of coffee, I came across an article in the *Los Angeles Times* about a Mexican who earned his citizenship some thirty-plus years after his death. This man died fighting for this country, and he wasn't a citizen? How could this be? I want to thank the *Los Angeles Times* and staff writer Sam Quinones for allowing me to use Juan Terrazas's story in this book. I also want to thank the Terrazas family for allowing me into their home, where they proudly shared stories of Juan's childhood, and to further honor Juan in this book.

Mexican immigrant Juan Terrazas died fighting in Vietnam. At last, Frank de la Vara makes his war buddy's dream come true. Juan Terrazas died serving the United States of America military, and now he is finally a citizen.

They knew each other only a short time, but Frank and Juan became as close as brothers when they served together in Vietnam.

Drafted into the Army, the two Mexican immigrants from Los Angeles, California, were so-called green-card soldiers who hoped to gain US citizenship when they returned to their adopted homeland.

De la Vara would realize his dream; Terrazas would not. The twenty-one-year-old Bronze Star recipient was killed in combat on July 9, 1969.

De la Vara never forgot his friend. For the next thirty-five years, he made annual visits to Terrazas's grave at Resurrection Cemetery in Montebello, California. Through failed relationships and periods of self-doubt, de la Vara found his emotional anchor in these pilgrimages.

Stirred by recent news reports of noncitizen troops being killed in Afghanistan and Iraq, de la Vara embarked on a mission to obtain posthumous citizenship for his fallen comrade. Support from Terrazas's family was crucial.

After one emotionally strained meeting with Terrazas's mother shortly after her son's death, de la Vara had lost contact with the family. Then in 2000, at the urging of his wife, he decided to reach out again.

He'd seen the flowers and the graveside mementos left at the cemetery by Terrazas's family. So on one of his regular visits, he left a note with his phone number in a plastic bag and tucked it into an empty vase.

Two weeks later, he received a call from Terrazas's youngest sister, Velia Ortega. Frank de la Vara was totally surprised. He didn't think anyone would call. They were really glad to hear from him.

With the help of the family and a local immigration official, also a Vietnam veteran, de la Vara obtained Juan Terrazas's citizenship papers. It took him four months and $80 to process the application.

On a Saturday, the 19th of November 2005, on a day that would have been Juan Terrazas's fifty-eighth birthday, de la Vara joined family and friends at Juan's graveside to mark the occasion.

This was the best Frank de la Vara could do for his buddy.

"The only honor we got was among ourselves," de la Vara said of his Vietnam brethren. Juan Terrazas was forgotten, and Frank did not want it to stay that way.

The Terrazas family moved to Los Angeles from Chihuahua, Mexico, in 1954. Juan Terrazas Sr. immediately found work at a tire factory in the evenings. His wife, Belia, worked days at a shop where bathing suits were made. They were old-school. They worked different hours so that one would always be home with the four children. Irma was the oldest. She was eight years old. Juan Jr. was six, Aurora was five, and the youngest was Velia at three. Coming into a new country and not speaking the language, the Terrazas family had a difficult transition. Through perseverance and time, they fulfilled the American dream. In 1961, Juan Sr. had saved enough money to buy their first home in Los Angeles. Belia Terrazas still lives in that same home.

While Juan Sr. was away at work, Juan Jr. assumed the duties as man of the house. The minute he was finished with his homework and English lessons, he began bossing the sisters around, getting them to do their homework and their share of the chores around the house. The little man of the house sensed the urgency of order by the long hours of work and exhaustion of Mom and Dad. As the children reached their teen years, Juan Jr. became very protective of his sisters. All potential dates were screened by him. One time a young man, described as a neighborhood punk, came calling on Juan's older sister Irma. Juan intervened and made it perfectly clear to the young man that his sister would not be going out on a date with him. Juan literally got in the boy's face. The young lad who was three years older and a foot taller than Juan never came around again.

Juan had always wanted to be a soldier when he grew up. In high school, he joined the Reserve Officer Training Corps and already had begun to map out his life's goals. He wanted to become a US citizen, marry his high school sweetheart, and attend college.

Not long after graduating high school, Juan was drafted into the Army. Worried for her son, Belia Terrazas urged her son to return to Mexico. He said that he would not be a draft-dodger. After all these years in the United States, he felt that it was not a time to run but rather a time to fight for a country that he would soon call his own.

Frank de la Vara and Juan Terrazas met at the Army induction center in Los Angeles in January 1968. They shared much in common. Born one day apart—Frank on the 18th of November 1947 and Juan on the 19th—both were immigrants and were the only boy in a family of girls.

After going through basic and advanced infantry training together at Fort Ord, California, Terrazas and de la Vara were assigned to Alpha Troop, 17th Calvary Regiment, 101st Airborne Division at Fort Campbell, Kentucky. In the spring of 1969, they arrived in Vietnam, more precisely, the Quang Tri Province near the Demilitarization Zone (DMZ). There they would see some of the fiercest fighting of the war.

Terrazas and de la Vara were in light infantry and patrolled the narrow A Shau Valley where the North Vietnamese (NVA) was funneling into South Vietnam. Their job was to go on reconnaissance missions, attract enemy fire, withdraw, and call in the regular infantry.

Of the twenty-four soldiers in their platoon, eighteen were foreign citizens, from countries such as Indonesia, Italy, Turkey, Mexico, and Canada. There was an article in the military newspaper, *The Stars and Stripes*, that dubbed them the United Nations Platoon. "It was kind of funny," recalls Frank de la Vara. "Most of us spoke with a different accent."

De la Vara also recalls a conversation he and Juan had at a USO show for the troops at base camp. "Terrazas suddenly turned to me and said, 'If anything happens to me, make sure that my mother and girlfriend get my stuff.'" Just a few days later, on the afternoon of July 9, 1969, Juan Terrazas died from wounds he received during a firefight in the A Shau Valley.

His family received letters he had written the week he died, reassuring them that everything was fine, as most soldiers did so as to not worry their loved ones. He thanked them for their mail and the packages they had been sending.

It was in October 1969 when the United Nations Platoon, along with some 650 other foreign-citizen military personnel, took the oath of US citizenship. "That's one of the reasons Juan became a soldier, to be a US citizen," said Aurora Carrera, Juan's sister.

When Frank de la Vara returned to Los Angeles, he and a buddy visited the Terrazas family. The visit was bittersweet. In her grief, Belia Terrazas said she wished it had been her son coming home instead of de la Vara. "It was a gut-wrenching experience standing there in front of Juan's mother and sisters with the feeling of guilt because I came home alive and Juan did not."

Frank de la Vara went on with his life. After separating from the Army, he took a job with a Southern California gas utility company, where he worked for the next thirty years until his retirement in 2000. He is currently married and has four children.

After all these years, Frank de la Vara never missed his visits to Juan Terrazas's grave. "I would sit there by myself and think about what was going on in my life and how it could have been different if Juan was still alive. Juan had such a positive influence in my life."

After Frank reunited with the Terrazas family, they agreed to meet every year on Juan's birthday and on Veterans Day at the cemetery.

Inspired by de la Vara's efforts, two of Juan's sisters, Irma and Velia, recently applied for citizenship. Velia said that she is also taking her seventy-five-year-old mother to do the same after more than fifty-one years in the United States. *"We should have filed for citizenship years ago in Juan's honor,"* said Velia. *"And for that I am sad."*

Juan Terrazas will be remembered on the Vietnam Memorial Wall as an honorable man who gave his all for a grateful nation.

Juan Luis Terrazas's name is located on the Vietnam Memorial Wall, panel 21W, line 91.

God be the music
Let me stop to listen to the symphony

If life be a song
Let me sing it with my whole heart

If love be a tear
Let me sob with tears of joy and sorrow
For God has a special vial just for me

If a soldier be the instrument of liberty
Let my voice ring out in honor to his memory

If a soldier sacrifices his life
Let it be for God, country, and his fellow man
For no greater love can be given

If death be the dirge to awaken our souls
Let Christ be our peace and our hope

If memories be the key to my heart
Let them be cherished
For those who have fallen,
Know the memories are alive and well
And kept next to my vial of tears

If honor and duty be the trumpets of angels
Let it be heard as the battle cry of heroes
Shouting from the heavens
With some called home to sit at the right hand of God

If courage be a heart's beat
Let its rhythm give him strength
And life for one more day

If gratitude be a light to the soldier's path
Let it shine brightly on his face
And warm him while he is away

If a prayer be the path
Let it travel straight to you

Dedicated to PFC Randall J. Gustafson
KIA, 02/14/1968, South Vietnam
by his sister Linda J. (Gustafson) Newlin

VESA JUHANI ALAKULPPI

After posting a memorial for Gary Keller on the Virtual Wall website, I browsed the site and was quite amazed at many of the memorials posted by family and friends. I thought to myself that these stories should be shared with as many people as possible. Vesa Alakulppi's memorial was one of them. I would like to thank Maija Harrington for allowing me to tell her story on the memory of her brother in this book.

Vesa Juhani Alakulppi was born in Rovaniemi, Finland, on April 23, 1941, to Olavi and Eevi Alakulppi during the Russo-Finnish War. Vesa's father was a captain in the Finnish Army. Vesa often spoke proudly of his father's exploits while fighting the Russian Army to a standstill. For his bravery, Olavi Alakulppi was awarded Finland's highest honor, the Mannerheim Cross, which is equivalent to our Medal of Honor. He was a Finnish national hero before the war as well because he placed first in the 1939 World Championship

Cross-Country Skiing. After a heroic fight however, the overwhelming might of the Soviet Union proved too much for Finland's small army, and the war ended in 1944.

Vesa's sister, Maija Harrington, recalls:

> *The events here are from my remembrances and as told to me by my mother, Eevi Kinnunen Alakulppi. After World War II, my father, Olavi Alakulppi, was placed in a prison camp in Finland because of his Finnish partisan, anti-Soviet activities, which I understand included obtaining and hiding weapons to be used in a hoped-for future revolt by Finland against the Soviet Union. One day Olavi faked having a bad toothache. He overpowered the guard who was escorting him to the dentist, and he escaped, eventually making his way to the United States and into the US Army. To this day I do not know how my father entered the United States. Both my mother and my father refused to tell me the details even when I repeatedly asked during my childhood and adulthood. Olavi's transit papers listed him as "stateless" in a way that led me to believe that he felt hurt and insulted by his homeland to his dying day.*
>
> *I was born in December 1945. Vesa was just four years old. We had a brother, Seppo, who was two years old when he died of pneumonia and the inability to get medical care during the war. Vesa's early childhood years, all the war years in Finland, must have been terribly frightening. My mother was very reluctant to discuss the war years with me, so I know very little.*
>
> *After Olavi's escape from prison, my mother, Vesa, and I stayed with my mother's sisters in Laurila and Tornio in Northern Finland. The Alakulppi family home and Olavi and Eevi's smaller home in Rovaniemi had been burned during the war. After Olavi's escape, my mother's activities were monitored by military guards who hoped to capture my father when he returned to his family. I am in awe of the courage Mother had during that time. To me, my mother was a war hero too.*
>
> *After a long period, Eevi said that the guarding had become relaxed so she began to plan her escape. While staying in Tornio near the Swedish border in early 1948, Eevi gathered her shopping bags and her two children, ages two and six. She eluded her guards and walked across the border to Haaparanta, Sweden, telling the border guards that she was there for a day of shopping. She then sought out the police station and asked for political asylum. The police cordially gave us a jail cell to sleep in. My mother did like to joke about how we spent our first night of freedom in jail.*

We spent nine months in Sweden while financial and other arrangements were made for us to join my father in America. Most of this time we were housed in a room in an "old folks home." I have no memories of our stay at this home. My mother said that I made myself very unwelcome there, with my two-year-old temper tantrums. The old folks complained about me a lot, and my mother was worried that we would be asked to leave. She said the old ladies loved Vesa. He must have been a very well-behaved six-year-old. I do have memories of a man with a mustache who would take me for walks during this time. I used to think the man was Mannerheim because he wore a uniform, so it is evident that there was talk of Mannerheim at our home. My mother later told me that he was one of the kindly policemen. Mother said that Vesa and I quickly became fluent in Swedish as well as Finnish.

I do have clear memories of sailing to America on the maiden voyage of the Swedish liner Stockholm, *which later became infamous for ramming the Italian ship* Andrea Doria *in the fog with much loss of life. We had a stateroom to ourselves with one bunk bed. All our possessions were in one steamer trunk. We left in December 1948 and arrived later in January 1949. We celebrated my third birthday on the ship. I thought it was a big party just for me, but it was a celebration for all December birthdays with lots of chocolate bars and hot cocoa for all.*

I definitely remember that the weather was terrible and the sea was fierce. I learned later from my mother that the ballast of the Stockholm *was not correct on its first voyage, which made the ship quite unstable, causing it to rock and roll inordinately in the heavy seas. Much of the time my mother was sick on the bottom bunk, which she shared with me, both the bunk and the sickness. Vesa had the top bunk. I have a spectacular memory of Vesa leaning over the top bunk to say he was going to be sick. Actually, he got sick before he could say it. All over my mother, myself, the bottom bunk, and the floor.*

Nevertheless, Vesa and I were not as sick as Mother, so we spent a lot of time playing together and looking at books on Vesa's top bunk. I believe Vesa was able to read to me at the time. My brother had an orange Swedish carved wooden horse that I liked, and he let me play with it. At one point, the ship lunged with such great force that I fell off the top bunk. Mom was able to break the fall, so I wasn't hurt, just frightened. I also recall a better day when my mom and I were able to go out on the deck. A great wave and sudden roll of the ship caused us to be knocked up against the ship's railing. My recollection from a three-year-old's perspective is that my mother saved me from falling overboard.

Our first day in the United States was in New York City, where we stayed in Harlem with a family who sponsored us for immigration purposes. At that time there was a Finnish immigrant community in Harlem. This would have been the first time that I met my father. It had been four years since Vesa saw his father. Interestingly, I have no memories of meeting my father. Vesa and I never talked about it. I do have memories of the apartment where we stayed. I remember their soft chenille bedspread that left funny marks on my brother's and my face. And I have vivid memories of the crisp winter walks along the riverside park.

Olavi Alakulppi had already been in the United States Army for nearly two years. He joined in 1947 with a small group of former Finnish Army officers as a buck private. Neither Olavi nor any of his fellow Finns spoke a word of English. Their expertise in cold weather survival was crucial to the Army. Their first assignment was a pre-Arctic trip to Castle Mountain near Mount Rainier, Washington. They were assigned to train the Army's Yukon Company in the basics of winter survival and over snow mobility. Olavi and the other Finns received refresher courses in English at night in preparation for teaching cross-country skiing the following day.

Olavi, Eevi, Vesa, and Maija were once again a family. A family of the United States Army. Olavi's and his fellow Finn's military background from Finland, along with their contribution to training soldiers in cold weather survival and their quick ability to learn the English language, had earned them a commission to the rank of captain, the same rank they held as Finnish officers. Vesa and Maija officially became "Army brats."

Vesa Alakulppi was not only a good and courageous man but also a wonderful big brother. From the time he was seven years old and I was just three, he took care of me. Wherever he went, so did I. "She's just my kid sister," he would say. Vesa would spend hours playing billiards with me at the Army recreational center before I could even reach over the table. He also took me along with him on his paper route, where my bedraggled presence was particularly helpful on collection day, even though my wildly inaccurate paper throws were not well appreciated.

When Vesa was ten years old and our parents were away to a military function, Vesa displayed great initiative by combing through our father's trouser pockets for change and finding three dimes. Leaving an IOU for thirty cents, he told me to get my bike, and we rode five miles to the town movie theater to see Lassie Come Home. *The movie kept repeating itself, so we stayed for the day's entire showings until our frantic parents spotted our bikes outside the theater at close to 11:00 p.m. But wow, that was a great movie, especially because I thought it was a real event currently happening before my eyes. This was still the pretelevision era, at least for our family. During future horror shows, Vesa was able to convince me that the movies were not real; otherwise he would have had to miss the movies.*

As we got older, Vesa continued to be responsible for the kid sister, even on many of his movie dates. His girlfriends generally did not appreciate my presence with the notable exception of his best high school sweetheart and future wife, Sharon.

Later, when I was a teenager, it was Vesa who went out to buy me a tube of Clearasil and taught me what it was and how to use it. He apparently had learned from his buddies years before, which turned out to be a good learning experience for me. Our parents of the "old country" didn't know of such cosmetic wonders.

At Plebe Christmas, when Vesa's ninth-grade kid sister (with her fifth-grade figure) wanted to take part in the dancing, he got a friend to dance with me as though I were the most glamorous girl of the evening.

Those are but a few fond memories to let you know that Vesa was pretty great even when he was a kid. I have always wished that everyone could have had a brother like Vesa.

Captain Olavi Alakulppi received his first overseas orders for an assignment to Germany in 1956. It was in Germany where Vesa began high school, attending the Nuremberg Dependent School, before transferring to Mainz where he met Sharon. Vesa was an honor student, ranking fourth in a class of 113 students, with a grade point average of 3.68. He also excelled in athletics, lettering twice in football while in Germany.

A couple of years later, the Alakulppi family returned to the United States. Olavi was stationed in Kansas. Vesa continued to excel in sports. He played on the Junction City basketball team that won the Central Kansas Conference Championship.

In March 1958, Vesa competed for and won a presidential appointment to the United States Military Academy. When a local reporter asked Vesa about his future aspirations, he replied, "I have been looking forward to a career as an Army officer all of my life." On the 7th of July, Vesa reported to the Man in the Red Sash in Old Central Area. After learning the rudiments of close order drill, he and his classmates were marched to Trophy Point and sworn in as new cadets in the class of 1959.

Vesa loved West Point, and he thrived in the demanding environment. A classmate recalled, "He was a quiet, honorable, top-drawer person. He really had a great mind and while he wouldn't normally admit it in public, he studied very hard to ensure he would always be prepared for class."

One of Vesa's roommates reflected upon his love for handball: "He was a fierce competitor, and he was pretty washed out when he returned to our room indicating that, win or lose, he had given it 100 percent. That's the way he approached everything."

Vesa often tutored classmates who were having academic problems. One classmate wrote, "I distinctly remember how he helped me prepare for the final exam in mechanics when I got turned out. So in no small measure, I owe Vesa big for the chance to complete my degree." Vesa's academic perseverance was rewarded in his first year by making the dean's list.

Graduation day finally arrived, and Vesa and his classmates were commissioned in the field house on June 5, 1963. He chose armor as his military occupational specialty, and after jump school at Fort Benning, Georgia, the new lieutenant reported to Fort Knox, Kentucky, for the armor officer basic course. Then he was off to Bamberg, Germany, where he served as Alpha Company Commander, Third Battalion, Thirty-Fifth Armor. In April 1966, Vesa and Sharon were married. A classmate remembers, "Those times we truly enjoyed being with Vesa and Sharon, having the fun of going out together on outings and taking short trips into the small German towns." In 1967, Vesa received orders for Vietnam with a stopover at the Jungle Warfare School in Panama.

Upon arriving in the Republic of South Vietnam, Captain Vesa Alakulppi was assigned to the Second Battalion, Third Infantry Regiment of the 199th Light Infantry Brigade. He was initially the Battalion S-2 (intelligence officer), but he volunteered to be a rifle company commander and was given C Company.

The troops of company C were skeptical of Captain Alakulppi. Why would this officer want to give up what was a relative safe position within the brigade to become an infantry platoon commander? This captain who has no combat experience. Captain Alakulppi was a quick study. It didn't take long before Vesa earned the respect and admiration of his men.

On March 28, 1968, Captain Alakulppi was awarded the Bronze Star Medal with combat V device for valor. The citation for that award reads as follows:

> *Captain Alakulppi distinguished himself by heroism in connection with ground operations against an armed hostile force in the Republic of Vietnam on 28 March 1968 while assigned to Company C, 2nd Battalion, 3rd Infantry, 199th Light Infantry Brigade. On that date, Capt Alakulppi was in charge of a company size search and destroy operation near the village of An Phu when the company encountered a well entrenched enemy force. The first platoon was*

immediately pinned down by an intense volume of enemy fire.
A sister platoon tried to aid the beleaguered platoon, but
it also became pinned down by the withering hostile fire.
During the ensuing battle, several men were mortally
wounded and it became apparent that the only way that the
enemy could be routed from their positions was through
tactical air strikes. Realizing this, Capt Alakulppi
ordered the company to withdraw across a river. As the
company was withdrawing, Capt Alakulppi and four other men
remained behind under the intense enemy fire to provide
protection. Disregarding his own personal safety, Capt
Alakulppi and his fellow comrades placed such effective
suppressive fire on the enemy that no further casualties
were sustained during the withdrawal. Because of his
courage and selfless concern for his fellow soldiers, the
lives of many men were saved. Capt Alakulppi's valorous
actions and devotion to duty were in keeping with the
highest traditions of the military service and reflected
great credit upon himself, the 199th Light Infantry Brigade
and the United States Army.

On May 14, 1968, Vesa's company was attacked by a superior force of North Vietnamese Army (NVA). After a furious battle, Captain Vesa Alakulppi was killed in action. A fellow company commander provided this account of the battle:

> Capt. Alakulppi, on losing communication with his strong point and receiving the report of enemy penetration from other bunkers, left his command post to tighten the remaining defenses and organize a counterattack. He went to the adjacent positions of the danger point, issued the orders to shift fires in order to contain the penetration, then started a personal reconnaissance of the situation. As he moved to a vantage point among the trees and irrigation ditches of the orchard, he was ambushed and killed.

For his actions, Captain Vesa Alakulppi was awarded the Silver Star Medal for valor posthumously. The citation reads as follows:

Captain Alakulppi distinguished himself by gallantry in
action while engaged in military operations involving
conflict with an armed hostile force on 14 May 1968 while

serving as Commanding Officer, Company C, 2nd Battalion, 3rd Infantry, 199th Light Infantry Brigade, in the Republic of Vietnam. On this date, Captain Alakulppi was in command of a ready reaction force consisting of one rifle platoon and a mortar section providing security for a large two-company base camp when an unknown size Viet Cong force attacked the perimeter with automatic weapons, small arms and rocket fire. Reacting immediately, Captain Alakulppi rallied his men to halt the enemy's advance. Realizing that because of adverse weather conditions, air support was not available, Captain Alakulppi repeatedly exposed himself to the intense enemy fire in order to direct supporting artillery fire close to his company's position. During the savage battle, without regard for his personal safety, he continually moved about the perimeter, encouraging his men and directing their fire. Realizing that his unit was isolated from friendly reinforcements, Captain Alakulppi continued to provide dynamic and aggressive leadership in the valiant defense of the base camp until he was mortally wounded by enemy fire. By his courageous actions, he inspired his men to greater efforts and enabled them to bring maximum suppressive fire against the Viet Cong force and repel the enemy attack. Captain Alakulppi's exceptional heroism and devotion to duty were in keeping with the highest traditions of the military service and reflect great credit upon himself, his unit and the United States Army.

On May 28, 1968, Vesa Juhani Alakulppi was laid to rest at the Evergreen Washelli Cemetery in Seattle, Washington. He was posthumously awarded the Silver Star Medal for bravery along with the Purple Heart Medal.

During the 1950s and 1960s, many of this country's teenagers and young adults were swarming the movie houses to feast their eyes on Hollywood heartthrobs such as Tab Hunter and Troy Donahue. These average actors with their handsome features made a living portraying characters like Vesa. Vesa portrayed himself throughout his life with dignity, courage, and love for his family and friends. He was also blessed with handsome features that would make Tab and Troy quite envious.

Vesa J. Alakulppi's name is located on the Vietnam Memorial Wall, panel 60E, line 007.

Heroes aren't athletes who set new sports records, or Hollywood actors who make "daring" films, or politicians who make bold promises. Heroes are people who place themselves at risk for the benefit of others.

—Oliver North

JAMES GLEN UPCHURCH

    Being a Marine and a subscriber to *Leatherneck*, the magazine for Marines, I sometimes come across an article that just grabs me by the heart and won't let go. "Putting Ghosts to Rest," written by *Leatherneck* staff writer and editor R. R. Keene in January 1999, is one of those stories. I would like to thank Mr. Keene and *Leatherneck* magazine for allowing me to use their story. I would also like to thank Kathy Upchurch for sharing with me memories of her loving husband, James Upchurch, and for allowing me to further honor her late husband in this book.

    I would also like to mention that he was with Echo Company, Second Battalion, Ninth Marines. I was also with Echo 2/9 but returned to the States several months before Lieutenant Upchurch arrived in country.

Dong Koi Mountain is one of those places where the Vietnamese do not go. It does not appear any more or less foreboding than neighboring Dong Ha Mountain and the surrounding hills of what was once Northern I Corps along the old Demilitarized Zone. But the local inhabitants believe it is haunted with the souls of unrested spirits.

As a rule, combat veterans don't put much stock in ghost stories, usually dismissing such tales as products of overactive imaginations. But every once in a while, someone will tell them of something unusual, which causes them to pause. Dong Koi is one such exception.

Twenty-five years after Reserve Second Lieutenant James Glenn "Jimmy" Upchurch made the ultimate sacrifice on that mountain, his widow, Kathy, stood at its foot, trying unsuccessfully to find someone to take her up on a tour. With her was Ed Henry, a former Navy corpsman who served with the Seventh Marine Regiment at Chu Lai and who is now a guide in Vietnam with Military Historical Tours of Alexandria, Virginia.

"We're not allowed in that area," he told her gently as they looked up the ridgeline. "It's an ancestral area the Vietnamese don't want disturbed." Their Vietnamese guide was less tactful. When he was asked to lead them up the ridge, his reply was a firm, "No!" So Kathy Upchurch stood at the foot of Dong Koi Mountain and prayed.

She had been an eighteen-year-old college freshman when, on a blind date, she met her future husband, an upperclassman who played football for East Central State University in Ada, Oklahoma. Jim Upchurch looked like an all-conference tackle that he was: broad shouldered, full of youthful power and confidence, and well-liked, but also a natural leader.

"He had a boy's sense of humor, direct with an easy laugh. And we became best friends," she said. "He was the first person in my life to ever fight for me," she added softly, without elaborating. He proposed on Saint Valentine's Day 1965, and they were married in June. Not quite two years later, he received his draft notice on January 28, 1967, his twenty-third birthday.

"Things were such then that he could have gotten a waiver, but he wasn't going to do that. His grandfather had been a Marine," Kathy said. She remembers the day when Jim and his friend, Larry Beck, came through the door and said in unison, "Guess what we did today?" They had signed up for Officer Candidates School. She can still hear that refrain today, tolling like a prophetic chorus, for both would die in Vietnam. *"Guess what we did today?"*

Second Lieutenant Upchurch's basic school class graduated in August 1968, and by September, he had orders to the Republic of South Vietnam. The couple had a month's leave to prepare for the separation.

Kathy had been teaching school while Jim attended OCS and TBS at Quantico, Virginia. They returned to his father's resort in Graford, Texas, where she could work as a backup fry cook, cabin cleaner, boat worker, and wait while Jim did his thirteen-month tour.

He wanted to make the Marine Corps a career, and she really wanted to have children. But decisions on both would have to wait. After Vietnam, there would be plenty of time for such things.

"I want to be buried in Lubbock, and here's who I want as pallbearers," Jim said out of the blue one night. He had pulled the car over to the side of the road and was calm when he spoke, but his statement had come without preamble. It was two days before he was to leave, and they were returning home from a party. It was too dark in the car for Kathy to see his face, but as he talked, she felt herself flush with fear, anger, and confusion. "Jimmy, why are you saying this?" She could feel tears welling up. "You're not going to be a hero or do anything to get hurt!"

"Kathy, you're a Marine officer's wife. You will always hold that chin up. And if anything happens, you're going to have to do it all," he said. "There'll be no tears in front of the family."

She thought about that as their car's headlights guided the way down a lonely ribbon of Texas road. She remembered it again when he left for Vietnam.

ON THE WAR FRONT

Vietnam in late 1968 was a time when the warring parties reassessed their strategies. The Third Marine Division launched a series of mobile firebase operations along South Vietnam's northern border area. The Americans, however, had come to realize that there was a limit to their participation in what had turned out to be America's longest war. The Corps, according to one Marine general, had "adopted the idea that we were in the postwar period." Maybe, but there was still a lot of killing to be done.

Second Lieutenant Upchurch found himself commanding Second Platoon of Echo Company, Second Battalion, Ninth Marine Regiment, Third Marine Division, in what was then Quang Tri Province. He considered himself lucky as his platoon sergeant, Douglas "Mack" McConnell, was considered to be one of the best. They hit it off and became friends in a situation where friendship is not easily earned nor quickly given. Kathy recalled Jim's letters speaking in glowing terms of Mack. In fact, the whole platoon seemed to take to their new lieutenant. Kathy received a Christmas letter from an anonymous member of his platoon that read, in part, "We feel he is one of the best lieutenants ever . . . He works with and for us. He takes great interest in our personal health and welfare. We are fortunate in having such a good lieutenant. On the other hand, he is fortunate in having a thoughtful wife who remembers us peons at

Christmas." (The letter is a reference to Christmas and other care packages she regularly sent to the platoon with notes of encouragement.)

More importantly, Lt. Upchurch proved to be a quick study and fast learner, essential traits in combat. In five months, he participated in eight major combat operations including Dewey Canyon. Operation Dewey Canyon took place in January 1969 in the A Shau Valley, an infamous North Vietnamese Army supply route. With the slap of AK-47 bullets overhead and the krumph of incoming mortar rounds forcing Second Platoon to hunker down into the red clay, Lt. Upchurch coordinated supporting-arms fire with cool skill and quiet confidence. He ordered a counterattack toward the heaviest point of contact, suffering casualties. The enemy soon took flight.

The young platoon commander was proving to be as tenacious as he was courageous. Later in February, one of his squads sprung a nasty ambush that killed those unlucky enough to be walking point for a large NVA force. Pressing his advantage, Lt. Upchurch and a fire team reinforced the ambush squad, and then he led the combined group in a vigorous assault. He was out front throwing grenades and firing his .45-caliber pistol. The NVA, bloodied and surprised, fell back. Later in February, Echo Company took on an NVA unit that was heavily armed with automatic weapons and rocket-propelled grenades. Upchurch deployed his platoon to ensure that all avenues of approach to their position were covered. When the shooting became heavy and the confusion of combat ensued, he stood exposed to heavy hostile fire and pointed out targets to his machine-gun squad.

Nobody in the platoon doubted their lieutenant's courage. Yet he confided in his letters to Kathy, "I'm scared every day." He also wrote of his concern for his fellow Marines and the fact that there were so many eighteen-year-olds. In one of his last letters, he wrote, "I really do believe there is a God, and I'm not afraid to die."

ON THE HOME FRONT

On March 25, Kathy had a dream that Jim was killed in combat. It upset her because she had recently written to him, asking to postpone for a month their planned rest-and-relaxation rendezvous in Hawaii due to a potential teaching job. She had been notified that the R & R dates had changed, but Jim hadn't yet replied.

They came to her door at 8:00 a.m., March 27. One was a Marine captain who was the recruiting officer out of Fort Worth. He was wearing the yellow-and-green and white-and-green ribbons that told her he was also a Vietnam veteran. Kathy saw them, and though she knew why they had come, she asked, "Is he a prisoner of war or missing in action?" The Marine captain with the ribbons from Vietnam said, "No." She told them, "You'd better come inside,"

Kathy was in jeans when they told her. She remembered that and remembered saying to them, "But he wasn't supposed to be there! We have our R & R planned. This can't be. This is not happening. This couldn't have happened to Jim. God wouldn't do this."

In a flush of painful emotion, it all ran in her mind. Their times together, his face, snapshot memories, trying to picture him again. Things only they knew. Then she remembered his words: "Kathy, you're a Marine officer's wife. If anything happens, you're going to have to do it all." She began to regain her control.

Jim had been an only child, and now there would be no children. Their marriage had lasted only three years and nine months. "It wasn't fair," she thought, and she was right. And certainly, nothing that followed seemed right.

Kathy had become close to Jim's father (his mother was deceased), and she called him first. "I lost Jim," she said. His father fell apart. As time went by, they drifted apart. The elder Mr. Upchurch became passive, then bitter, and threw himself into his work. She would see him only a few more times before he died in 1988.

For Kathy, Jim's death was initially met with denial. But there was another setback. Four days after his death, Jim's last letter to her arrived. In it he expressed disappointment with her for wanting to move their planned R & R dates back. "Is teaching more important than me?" he'd asked. She was devastated by yet another powerful emotion: guilt.

At the funeral, she remembered his admonition: "There'll be no tears in front of the family." And there were none. But there was no closure either, she said, explaining that it was, of course, a closed-casket funeral. "If I could have just seen a hand or something."

Kathy later learned the details of how her husband died in a letter from Sgt. Mack, written May 1, 1969, at Quang Tri.

Dear Mrs. Upchurch,

I'm sorry I've been so long in answering the letter you addressed to our platoon. I was your husband's platoon sergeant, and I like to consider myself also as one of his friends . . . I'm sure I can speak for all of the platoon when I say we share your loss of not only a damn good platoon commander, but also a fine human being. The rapport he established was one of the finest I've seen in my career. You asked for details surrounding your husband's death. I'll try to tell you. The NVA had been hitting route

9 with mortars and sniper fire. The battalion had wanted the 2nd and 3rd platoons of Echo and two platoons of Fox Company to sweep the hills and clear the enemy . . . It was decided that the lieutenant would take the "company minus" as the company commander, a job we all felt he was qualified to do. I was to take over his job as the 2nd platoon commander. We had seen signs of the enemy, but it appeared that he was leaving the area. The company felt that it would be an uneventful operation, including the lieutenant. We all felt we were in good hands while "Mr. Upchurch" was in charge. The next day, the 3rd platoon was moving out first, and the command post and mortars (the lieutenant's group) were going to be moving up with the 2nd platoon. It was at this time the enemy first opened up with automatic weapons on the column. They were on our objective and on another hill to the right from which we were taking automatic and machine-gun fire. Just before we made the assault, the lieutenant told me, "Give 'em hell, Sgt. Mack." It was his platoon, and I knew he was wishing he could make that assault with us. It was what he had been training us for so long. Well, we took the hill without a friendly casualty. He was really proud of us. I was talking on the radio with him, and he had maneuvered the "company minus" into taking both the objective and the other hill. He told me that the enemy was on the run and was going into Fox company's blocking force. We then set in and were preparing to take a break. We could see Mr. Upchurch and his radio operator on the hill to our left. Then it happened. The enemy started dropping mortars on the hill the lieutenant was on. The first round they fired was too far over the target they had picked. We, the 2nd platoon, could see it hit and tried to tell them by radio to take cover, for it seems they didn't see it. However, the enemy had "keyed out" our radio frequency, and we had no communication with them. The next round was only a moment later, and we could see it had hit our lieutenant and his radio operator [who would survive]. Then the enemy started dropping mortar rounds all over their hill which we had just taken. The corpsman was right there to help, but Mr. Upchurch had been slain immediately . . . We were able to get the killed and wounded out by chopper. War, Mrs. Upchurch, is a horrible nightmare. It makes old men out of young boys. I saw some of those "old men" in the lieutenant's platoon crying that day. There is no doubt that they had lost a platoon commander (whom) they loved as a leader and as a man. The loss of our lieutenant is one we cannot or will not forget. We all share your grief for the loss of one we all admired and respected. We will always be proud to say we served under him. Most of the old platoon is gone now. There are only about 10 of us left. Some have gone home, some have been wounded, *some died, but those who have gone carry the memory of their lieutenant and the fine things he did for them as a platoon and as individuals. We all suffer losses in these hard times. All I can say after, is the way I've found to help ease some of the pain I've encountered, is faith through God in prayer. I'll close for now.*

My deepest regret,

Sgt. Mack

She never heard from Sgt. Mack again. For the next few weeks and months, she listened to people offering sympathy as she wrapped things up. She had come to the conclusion that the Marines had handled things badly, from sending an officer who was inexperienced in casualty assistance to shipping her husband's body in what she believed was a less-than-timely fashion. "Jim's death and what was happening to me: it all just wasn't real. It came home to me when his personal effects arrived. His wedding ring and a crucifix were the first things I saw, and I knew it was final." She wept alone.

She had their wedding bands made into a ring, which she kept, and made a scrapbook for Jim's father that included the Purple Heart and two Bronze Star citations. "I threw away Jim's letters because I didn't have a child to pass them on to." Then she tried to start over.

However, one thought lingered. "Is teaching more important than me?" And each time she heard his words, she always answered, "If I hadn't asked for the R & R date to change, he'd still be alive."

It haunted her. She went back to school and earned a master's degree in physical education. Then she wanted to be a nurse but ended up teaching public school in Springfield, Virginia. She dated a few military men and four years later remarried. That marriage lasted six years.

"If I hadn't asked for the R & R date to change, he'd still be alive," she kept thinking. Looking back, Kathy said that it was that thought, more often than not, that sabotaged her relationships with others. Depression set in.

"I was becoming a number-one bitch who needed to see a shrink." She did, and he suggested that she visit Vietnam. She also discovered the Gold Star Wives of America Inc., a nonprofit national military widows' service organization that took its name from an old custom in World War II. Families of those serving in the military back then were issued Blue Star flags, which were proudly displayed in their windows while they waited for a loved one to return from the war. Sometimes the wait was in vain, and the family replaced the blue flag with a Gold Star flag, signifying a member of their family had been killed in action. In this group, Kathy found others who understood how she felt. It was a combination of friends, old and new, who encouraged her to bring things to closure in a journey to Vietnam.

In 1994, on what would have been Kathy and Jim Upchurch's twenty-ninth wedding anniversary, she arrived in Hanoi. A few days later, with maps provided by Marines who had known her husband, she was near the Seventeenth Parallel at the foot of Dong Koi Mountain, looking up toward where her husband had been killed.

Kathy chose a sapling and hung a small wooden folk angel on it to approbate the spirits and in remembrance of not only Jim but all who fought and died there.

"I believe that I heard Jim's voice, and he told me, 'I am at peace. I knew you would come for God and I have been guiding you . . . It is now time for you to be at peace.'"

"I didn't hear anything," said guide Ed Henry. "But I'll tell you what. It was like being in a bad place. The Vietnamese guides just left. While we were there, I got a feeling of something not being right, sort of like just before an ambush we once walked into near Chu Lai. It was like we were surrounded by people watching us. It was just spooky."

Whether or not Jim spoke to her does not really matter to anyone but Kathy Upchurch. For her, the trip was a catharsis, purging most of her emotional demons. "I thank God for letting me go to Vietnam. The pain, which had been deeply buried, all came to the surface. I realize that Jim died doing what he wanted to do. He wanted to go serve and be who he was. I had to face up to that," she said.

She also came to grips with her feelings about the Corps. "I had a love-hate relationship with the Marine Corps. You love the strength and leadership and the good it instills in Marines. I hated it because back then, it didn't seem to value the family enough. But there isn't a Marine I've ever met who wasn't protective of me."

She returned to Vietnam again in March 1998 because she discovered that she liked the country and its people. While there, the mayor of Dong Ha, hearing that she was a war widow, told her, "I am sorry about your husband. I served in Dong Ha. I wish you happiness, long life, and good health." A teacher, Mrs. Ng Thi Cam Hong, also asked her, "Do you hate us?" The question brought Kathy Upchurch to tears. "Hate had never entered my heart concerning the Vietnamese people. I was raised in the Christian belief that unconditional love was a better method of solving problems. Anger yes, hatred no."

She looked in the direction of the mountain where her husband had been killed so many years ago. "Climbing that mountain isn't important anymore," she said. "I've learned that life is an ongoing process, and you have to roll with it, and maybe I'm supposed to help someone else get through hard times."

While she still thinks now and then of the man she has loved for so long, she admitted that it is sometimes difficult to remember Jim's smile, laughter, and brown eyes. "How dark brown they were," she whispered and wished she had never thrown his letters away.

James Glenn Upchurch's name is located on the Vietnam Memorial Wall, panel 28W, line 041.

More than a Name on the Wall

I saw her from a distance
as she walked up to the Wall
In her hand she held some flowers
as her tears began to fall
and she took out pen and paper
as to trace her memories
and she looked up to heaven
and the words she said were these . . .

She said, Lord, my boy was special,
and he meant so much to me
and oh I'd love to see him
just one more time you see
all I have are the memories
and the moments to recall
so Lord could you tell him
he's more than a name on a Wall . . .

She said he really missed the family
and being home on Christmas Day
and he died for God and country
in a place so far away.
I remember just a little boy
playing war since he was three
but Lord this time I know
he's not coming home to me

And she said Lord my boy was special,
and he meant so much to me
and oh I'd love to see him
but I know it just can't be
So I thank you for my memories
and the moments to recall
but Lord could you tell him,
he's more than a name on a Wall

Lord could you tell him
he's more than a name on a Wall . . .

Lyrics by the Statler Brothers

JOHN HARVEY CARSON

A few years ago, I got a call from a man named John Carson. He tells me that I served with his son in Vietnam. I was quite surprised by the call. He told me that he got my name and number off the 2/9 website under those that served with Echo Company, Second Battalion, Ninth Marines. I told him that I remember a Lt. Carson, who was my platoon commander, but I did not remember his first name. He confirmed that his son was my platoon commander. He also told me that his son, John H. Carson, was killed in June 1968. That I didn't know. It's funny how emotions can sucker-punch you even after forty years.

A new friendship was born after that call. While traveling across the country in 2004, I had the pleasure of being the guest of Mr. and Mrs. John William Carson in their Spokane home.

In the Carson family, the apple never fell far from the tree. John Harvey Carson was born in East Stroudburg, Pennsylvania, on the 26th of August 1946. His mother was Elizabeth M. Pysher of Bangor, Pennsylvania. His father is John William Carson, originally from Hershey, Pennsylvania, now living in Spokane, Washington.

On June 23, 1942, John William Carson enlisted in the Army Air Corps, the same day he received his high school diploma. John's twin brother, Eugene, also entered the Army Air Corps. After many months of extensive training, John was assigned the position of tail gunner on a B-17. In early August of 1943, John arrived at his first overseas assignment with the Second Bomb Group, Ninety-Sixth Squadron. A B-17 unit stationed near Tunis, North Africa. Eugene was also a tail gunner assigned to the Eighth US Army Air Corps in England from 1943 to 1945.

John and Eugene's father, Thomas W. Carson, originally from Beckley, West Virginia, died from the aftereffects of phosgene gas poisoning suffered during World War I. His early death at the age of twenty-seven left their mother, Esther H. Carson, with twin boys only one year old. Eugene remembers, "Mother never remarried. Every day she took time to look at our father's picture hung on the wall above the fireplace mantle. She often told us, *'Your father always said he never wanted you boys to be soldiers.'* She cried during high school graduation night when John told her of his enlistment as she had undoubtedly cried when Tom Carson died. Again, her tears were to no avail. The country was at war. My twin brother, John, had heard the bugle call. Now I too was hearing the echo of the bugle."

John William Carson recalls his experience with the Ninety-Sixth:

> My first twenty-three missions were in the tail, the last five would be as a radio operator. As a tail gunner, I had the comfort of being able to fight back. But the radio operator position was not a very defensible position from a standpoint of having a chance to do any real shooting. On the B-17F model, the radio operator removed an overhead hatch at the rear of the position and then brought his 50-caliber gun out on a rail to fire out of the opening. The gun was mounted on a ring and would traverse vertically and horizontally but with a very limited field of fire and limited ammunition. On my final mission, this gun nearly came to be my undoing. I manned this new position with my new crew on the B-17F named What a Tomato. It was piloted by Lt. Dave Rohrig. Lt. Lloyd Haefs was the bombardier. T.Sgt. Dave Hiskey was the engineer. S.Sgt. Louis Crawford was the lower ball gunner. S.Sgts. Horner and Walter Chesser were the waist gunners. S.Sgt. Corely was in the tail. Some

of the other names are blank to me. Those were my crew members with whom I flew my last missions."

It seemed like I was assigned to a crew destined to hard luck. Or perhaps the missions were getting harder. Of the five missions I flew with them, each mission should have been a sign of impending disaster. Only we all too often fail to see the signs. We almost went down on our fourth mission. We were flying lead when German fighters jumped us. S.Sgt. Corley was wounded. The fighters went to work in earnest, riddling the plane with canon fire. They took the right wing tip off all the way to the airelon and also damaged the hydraulic system to say nothing about the jagged foot-long holes all back through the fuselage. The plane looked like a sieve and developed a severe vibration. We were out of formation and battling to save our butts when our fighters arrived and pulled the bacon out of the fire. One of our wingmen rejoined us and was quite encouraging. He would tell the pilot, *'I don't think you are going to make it, Dave.'* Words we all wanted to hear. Despite our wingman's dire predictions, our pilot did not listen to him and never gave the order to bail out. I was glad. Although it was touch and go, we did make it back.

Our next time out would be on a plane named Eager Beaver. It was a B-17F that had been on many missions and scored many kills. Well-known in the Ninety-Sixth, the Eager Beaver had been used before by the squadron commander Maj. Buck Caruthers. Our first and final mission we were assigned on the Eager Beaver was a strike on the Aloysius Airdrome at Athens, Greece. The Aloysius mission was supposed to be an easy target. It turned out to be anything but. As we approached the target, heavy and extremely accurate 88 mm flak started to rise, and we took some bad licks. We were lead plane at an altitude of 21,500 feet approaching the indicated point (IP), the point where the bombardier takes control of the plane. Since the bombardier needs a steady plane to aim the bomb drop, no evasive maneuvers can be made from the IP until the bombs are away. As we approached the IP, the flak grew heavier. Just as we made the IP, all hell broke loose. I heard the pilot ask the bombardier how he was doing. Haefs answered, *'I am going to let them go any second, Dave.'* I then reached for the front radio room door, which opened onto the bomb bay, so I could advise when all bombs were clear off the plane. At that instant, I found myself holding the handle and no door. We had taken a severe hit under the aircraft, in the area of the bomb bay. I turned to the rear of the plane and grabbed for my mike cord to advise the pilot of possible damage. As I did so, another 88 burst over and straight behind the vertical stabilizer, just aft of the plane. The rear radio room door splintered and struck me in the face. A third flak burst had struck us at the waist door, severing the entire tail from the rest of the plane. I never saw the blast. Immediately afterward I could see someone struggling among the dust and smoke in the waist as the plane rolled over on its back. We were at 21,500 feet and headed down. The engines of the plane were screaming. I found myself looking at the ground through the top of the plane, straddling the radio gun, with both feet hanging out of the slipstream. There was no way I could get out. Realizing that I was trapped, I tried to cover my fear by fainting, but it didn't work. Somehow I found the strength to extricate myself and went back through the waist and bailed out the end of the falling bird. I can still recall the moan of the engines, the jagged metal of the torn fuselage, and the jerk I gave the ripcord on my backpack. Now I was floating in the air. Below bombs were going off; above 88s were exploding. Sounds of bullets and flak whistling by convinced me that I was being shot at. I spilled the chute to become a tougher target. It oscillated so violently that not only did I become sick, I worried that the chute would turn all the way over and collapse. That passed and I then began to take stock. I had no serious wounds, just some surface wounds and metal splinters from the door. As I neared the ground, I looked down and could see that I was going to land in a field. I also spotted two German soldiers with fixed bayonets approaching. The Germans did not approach as fast as the ground. Hitting the ground was like jumping off a two-story building. I never realized it would be so rough. The Germans immediately got to my position and demanded that I get to my feet. After taking the time to stay on bended knee and thank God for being spared, I stood up and entered captivity. From that moment on December 20, 1943, I began my life as a prisoner of war at the hands of the German Army.

After several weeks of solitary confinement and persistent interrogation, John William Carson was assigned to Stalag Luft VI in Hydekrug, East Prussia. In mid-July 1944, it became necessary to evacuate Stalag Luft VI due to the Russian advance. He then went to Stalag Luft IV, near Gross, Tychon, Poland. In February 1945, the Soviet offensive was rapidly pushing toward Stalag Luft IV. The German high command decided that it was necessary that the POWs be evacuated and moved into Germany, but by that stage of the war, German material was at a premium, and neither sufficient railcars nor trucks were available to move prisoners. Therefore, the decision was made to move the Allied prisoners by foot in a forced road march. It was the coldest winter Europe had experienced in many years. Around 2,500 prisoners covered nearly 500 miles in 86 days. A number of American POWs on the march did not survive. Others suffered amputations of limbs and appendages while many more endured maladies that remained or will remain with them for the rest of their lives. They endured unbelievably inhumane conditions—the men from Stalag Luft IV walked, limped, and in some cases, crawled onward until they reached the end of their march, with their liberation by the American 104th Infantry Division on April 26, 1945. The surviving POWs, including John William Carson, choked back sobs of joy; their incredible journey was coming to a happy ending.

Within two weeks, John William Carson arrived at Fort Dix, New Jersey, upon which time he took a quick physical, received a uniform issue, some back pay, and a well-deserved thirty-day leave.

John remembered how excited he was to reunite with his new bride after being away for sixteen months:

> I pulled into Van Buren Station in Chicago where my wife, the former Ms. Dorothy Spinka, and her mother met me. We got in the car and she kept sobbing. I told her to not cry. I am fine, just skinny. She announced she had something to tell me. I had been reported killed in action for over a month, and in the meantime she had married an old high school sweetheart. I was speechless. I went home to my mother and I believe that the rest of my leave was spent in a state of shock. After my leave, I returned to Miami Beach for processing; either reenlistment or separation. Being very bitter I blamed the Army for my marital demise. I opted for the latter. I bought a Harley Davidson motorcycle and bummed around the country for a year and a half. That's how long it took me to realize that I missed the Army.

John William Carson returned to the Army in 1947 as a staff sergeant. In 1949 he applied for Officer Candidates School and was commissioned a second lieutenant in July of that same year. He served this great country for over thirty years, which included duty in Korea and Vietnam.

During his hiatus from the Army, John met Elizabeth Pysher. After a short romance, they immediately got married. Their first child was John Harvey Carson. John Harvey was raised as an Army brat and spent most of his youth in San Antonio. His father was stationed at nearby Kelly Air Force Base. John Harvey graduated from Jefferson High School in San Antonio, Texas, where he excelled in the Army ROTC. He was cadet sergeant major in his senior year and was awarded the prestigious Bentencourt Medal, which traditionally had gone to the corps commandant.

John Harvey attended the University of Texas, Austin. After one year, he decided to enter the Marine Corps. He attended boot camp at the Marine Corps Recruit Depot in San Diego, California. He completed boot camp as the series honor man and led the graduation parade in Marine dress blues. Shortly after boot camp, he was accepted for Officer Candidates School, which he also completed with high honors.

Second Lieutenant John Harvey Carson was trained to be an infantry leader, which subsequently led to his assignment in Vietnam. In early January 1968, Lt. Carson was assigned to Echo Company, Second Battalion, Ninth Marine Regiment, Third Marine Division as the Second Platoon commander.

Lt. Carson was familiar with the Ninth Marines' rich history. They had distinguished themselves during World War II and had already distinguished themselves in Vietnam since their landing at Da Nang in 1965. They set precedents that Marines and units throughout Vietnam would emulate, precedents in protecting Vietnamese rice crops, in fighting the Viet Cong, and in the heavy fighting with the North Vietnamese main force units in and near the DMZ. From their initial landing until early 1967, they operated in areas south of Da Nang amidst a large Vietnamese population. Then they moved north to Dong Ha where, for more than a year, they made headlines in operations such as Hickory, Kingfisher, Buffalo, and Kentucky in "Leatherneck Square" and places like Con Thien, Camp Carroll, and Gio Linh.

One significant note during its many operations throughout I Corps is that, at one time or another, the regiment was in operational control of virtually every single battalion in the First and Third Marine Divisions.

Throughout the remaining months of 1966 and early 1967, the Ninth Marines conducted numerous search and clear operations to search out the enemy while strengthening their civic action programs to secure relations with the Vietnamese people, and free the people of constant threat of Viet Cong terrorism.

After the Ninth Marines moved to Dong Ha in April 1967, they became involved in some of the bitterest fighting of the war, in areas near Khe Sanh, Gio Linh, and Con Thien. Near Con Thien, Marine Leathernecks killed 991 enemy soldiers during Operation Buffalo while being almost constantly bombarded by enemy artillery and rockets. Later in September of that year, the outpost at Con Thien near the DMZ came under one of the heaviest artillery poundings of the war, lasting for twelve straight days. Elements of the regiment who manned the outpost during the siege turned back several NVA assaults, inflicting heavy casualties on the attackers. With the aid of air and artillery support, the Ninth Marines turned the enemy attack into an enemy disaster.

When Lt. Carson took over as Second Platoon commander, he made it clear to his Marines that he was aware of their accomplishments and their sacrifices. He told his men that he was proud to be fighting alongside the fiercest military force on the planet. He was sincere and compassionate. He would never give an order that he himself would not do. Lt. Carson was a quick study to the men, the Vietnamese, and his surrounding environment. It didn't take long for him to gain the respect and admiration from the men that served under him as well as his senior officers.

HM3 Dennis Chaney was a Navy corpsman assigned to Lt. Carson's Second Platoon. Doc Chaney recalls his first day in Vietnam:

> I was terrified when I arrived at Camp Carroll, the Marine combat base near the village of Cam Lo. The words of the rawboned, tanned Marine at the airport at Phu Bai had given me more than just a bit of apprehension. He had overheard me talking to Gene DeWeese, my buddy who had gone through corps school with me, as we waited to board the C-130 that would take us to Dong Ha on our way north to join the Marines at Carroll. It was obvious that he had been in Vietnam long enough to know what he was talking about. "Two-Nine? That's the Blood Bucket Battalion." "Blood Bucket Battalion?" "Yeah. They've lost more men than anyone else. They're a real meat grinder. They're in the worst part of the whole damn country, up north, right near the DMZ."
>
> And from what I could see, it appeared he was right. This definitely was a combat zone. Surrounding the main area of hard-backed tents were artillery pits, concertina wire laced with claymore mines, wooden watchtowers, bunkers, and red dirt. The amount of sandbags that had been filled and stacked was tremendous. Everything was fortified. The Marines didn't build a place like this unless they expected bad things to happen. And where bad things happen, a man needs an abundance of luck, or maybe a guardian angel. Mine appeared when I reported to Echo Company.
>
> "Anything you need, Doc, just ask," said Lieutenant Carson, my new platoon commander. "We take care of our docs. Just do your job and take care of my men. Above all, Doc, don't sweat the program. I'll take care of you. You'll be just fine."
>
> I felt much better after Carson's friendly welcome. He seemed like a capable fellow and one that was sympathetic to the needs of his men. For the first time, I began to relax a bit. He didn't seem worried and appeared to have the situation under control.

Former Lance Corporal John Foster remembers his first meeting with Lt. Carson:

In January 1968, the Second Platoon of Echo Company was sent to Delta-5, which was just north of Camp Carroll. D-5 was a small post alongside an old French fort. Our job was to give temporary support to an ARVN unit. One day while at D-5, an ARVN officer approached me and asked if I would sell him an extra pair of jungle utilities (fatigues). I told him that he could have them for $15. When he returned with his money, I gave him the utilities. This little shit gave me monopoly money. I told him that the money was no good, and he insisted that it was. He actually showed me the "In God We Trust" printed on the play money. I yelled at him to give me back the utilities, and he ran. I chased after him right up to Lt. Carson. Lt. Carson excused the ARVN officer and looked at me with a "What the hell are you doing?" look. "Sir, that ARVN ripped me off. He gave me monopoly money for a set of utilities." "That's too bad, Marine. You have all been told to never barter with the Vietnamese, including the ARVN. You can chalk it up as a $15 lesson." I was pissed. Pissed at the little shit that ripped me off, pissed at Lt. Carson, and mostly pissed at myself because I did know better.

Not long after the utility incident, we had received mail. I was sitting next to my bunker, reading a letter from my mom, when Lt. Carson sat next to me and put his hand on my shoulder. "Is everything okay back home?" he asked. "Yes, sir." It was then that I learned more about the lieutenant. He showed a genuine interest in me by wanting to know where I was from and a little bit about my background. He also told me about himself and about growing up in Texas. It wasn't just me he showed an interest in. He was that way with the whole platoon. There was a likeable easiness about him, yet he was firm in his orders. Perhaps one of the reasons Lt. Carson was well liked is because of his youthfulness. The lieutenant and all the young Marines had the same interests like cars, music, and pretty girls. Even though he was married and true to his wife, a picture of a pretty girl would always bring a smile to his face.

Most officers and senior enlisted men didn't get that close to the troops because so many young Marines died in their presence, and they knew more would die. Maybe that was a good thing. Lt. Carson didn't feel that way. He was more optimistic.

Immediately after returning to Camp Carroll in late January, two other Marines and I were ordered to field incineration duty, also known as field sanitation but commonly known as burning the shitters. For the life of me, I could not imagine what I did to deserve burning someone else's shit. The other two Marines didn't seem to mind. After moving the waste buckets toward them so that one could pour diesel fuel and the other could torch the waste, I could see why they didn't mind. They were smoking pot. Two happy Marines burning shit and getting high. They had no worries because no one was going to get close enough to the job to see what they were doing, and besides, the foul smell very well covered the aroma of the marijuana. While we were burning the shitters, Lt. Carson entered an officer's screened outhouse with reading material in hand. The two high Marines went to their tents and retrieved a couple of white illumination star clusters. They were giggling like a couple of high school pranksters. They took aim at the outhouse occupied by Lt. Carson. Two direct hits. That shitter lit up like a 4th of July sky. Carson ran out with his trousers around his ankles, yelling, "Incoming!" The two Marines were rolling on the ground and laughing their asses off. I stood there with my mouth open in shock. I couldn't believe what I had just witnessed. I also couldn't believe that the lieutenant could run so fast with his ankles bound with his pants. It didn't take the lieutenant long to realize that there was no incoming. After he got himself dressed, he started walking toward me. He demanded to know who was responsible for the attack on his outhouse. I was at a loss for words. I just froze. The two Marines immediately got rid of the evidence by throwing the empty cluster tubes into a waste bucket. They told Carson that they believed a couple of soldiers from the Army side of Camp Carroll were responsible for the act. "The Army had been known for such pranks in the past," they had told him. Lt. Carson wasted no time going to the Army post to make inquiries. I then joined the two Marines for the best laugh I had while in Vietnam.

Former Marine Alva Moring had this to say about Lt. Carson:

I served with Lt. Carson as his platoon messenger from January through March of 1968. I was just a lance corporal, but he became more than my platoon commander. He became my friend. He and I had served under fire together and developed a very trusting fellowship in such a short period of time. One night, when our position was being hit with heavy enemy fire, our platoon was to fall out as a reactionary force. Lt. Carson knew that my tour in Vietnam was near the end, so he told me to stay behind in case the captain needed anything. I told him, "No, sir, I am going with you." He knew what I meant, and he did not order me to stay behind. This was the respect and admiration I had for him. To stand beside him, to carry out and perform whatever his orders.

Lt. John Harvey Carson was awarded the Bronze Star Medal with combat V device for heroic action on the 6th of April 1968. The citation reads as follows:

For heroic achievement in connection with operations against the enemy in the Republic of Vietnam while serving as a Platoon Commander with Company E, Second Battalion, Ninth Marines, Third Marine Division. On 6 April 1968, Second Lieutenant Carson's platoon was the lead element of a helicopter-borne force consisting of another platoon and the company command post assigned to recover a Marine killed during a previous reconnaissance mission near Hill 190 in Quang Tri Province. Almost immediately upon landing, his platoon came under heavy mortar fire from entrenched North Vietnamese Army on the hill and emplacements in the surrounding terrain. Ignoring the danger to his life, he repeatedly exposed himself to exploding enemy rounds as he deployed his men to secure the landing zone for the arrival of the remainder of the force. He then skillfully maneuvered his men through the increasingly hostile mortar and artillery fire to reach and secure the crest of the hill. Completely disregarding his own safety, he personally supervised and assisted in carrying wounded Marines from the fire-swept slopes to the landing zone, returning each time across the hazardous area to direct the actions of the men on the hill top. When informed that both the company commander and executive officer had become casualties, he immediately assumed command, rapidly assessed the situation and established defensive positions. Organizing the command group to provide security, he then directed the movement of the platoons to the landing zone for retraction. Only

after ensuring that all the casualties had been
medically evacuated and the remainder of the company
embarked did he board the last helicopter and depart
the area. Second Lieutenant Carson's courage, bold
initiative and selfless devotion to duty were in
keeping with the highest traditions of the United
States Naval Service.

On the 5th of June 1968, Lt. John Harvey Carson was leading a convoy of new replacements out to the field when it was ambushed. The jeep in which Lt. Carson was riding took a direct hit from a rocket-propelled grenade (RPG). The lieutenant and his driver were killed instantly.

Our doc, HM3 Dennis Chaney, remembers hearing of Lt. Carson's death:

While crossing the Cam Lo River, Harry Thomas, our radioman, fell into the river when his equipment on his pack shifted. We scanned the surface of the water frantically, waiting for his head to bob up, but it didn't. After several diving attempts to look for Harry, I found his body wedged under a rock. With the help of other Marines, we pulled him up onto the bank of the river. There was no pulse. Neither mouth-to-mouth nor heart massage would help. Harry was dead. Harry was also my friend, and it was hard to accept the fact that he died in such a manner in the middle of this war. I took Harry back to the Battalion Aid Station in Cam Lo. When I arrived, there was a lot of activity. A helicopter had been shot down on its approach to the tiny base and burned on impact. The pilot's body had been brought in and was badly charred. The horrible smell of burnt flesh permeated the air, assailing my nostrils and clinging to me like a nightmare I couldn't wake up from. Between losing Harry and seeing the pilot, I was losing it. I just couldn't take it anymore. While I stood there trying to hang on to what little sanity I had left, the battalion surgeon walked up. "Chaney, I've got some bad news." "I don't need any more bad news, sir." "A jeep was knocked out yesterday afternoon by an RPG round," he informed me as gently as he could. I had to ask the question but was afraid to ask. Finally, I did. "Who was in the jeep?" "Lieutenant Carson." "No! It can't be!" I sobbed. I felt like I had been hit in the head with a brick. Not Lieutenant Carson! The man who had taken extra measures to take care of me all the time I was with his platoon, my friend, my guardian angel—it couldn't be! He was my officer, and I was his doc. I had my pick of C rations, my choice of where I slept, anything I needed to do my job. He saw that I had the best of what could be offered. He even assigned his radioman to be my security, sponsor, and protector. Lieutenant Carson not only took care of me, he took care of all his men in the same manner.

The company commander who'd demanded the folly on Hill 37 had finally been relieved, and Lt. Carson, being the senior lieutenant in the company, had taken temporary command while we waited for a new captain. As such, the convoy escort had fallen to him.

John Harvey Carson's name is located on the Vietnam Memorial Wall, panel 60W, line 016.

When You Are a Soldier

When you are a soldier, I will be your shield
I will go with you into the battlefield
When the bullets start to fly
Take my hand . . . hold on tight
I will be your shield
'Cuz I know how it feels
When you are a soldier

When you're tired of runnin', I will cheer you on
Look beside you and you'll see . . . You're not alone
And when your strength is almost gone
I'll carry you until you're strong
I will be your shield
'Cuz I know how it feels
When you are a soldier

I will be the one that you can cry your song to
And my eyes will share your tears
Then when the enemy surrounds you
You'll see that love will quench your fears

When you are lost and lonely, I will hold the light
I will help you find the way through the night
I'll remind you of the truth
Help keep the flame alive in you
I will be your shield
'Cuz I know how it feels
When you are a soldier

Deborah Ann Alamo

GABRIEL R. ALAMO

Another thanks to the Virtual Wall. While browsing their site, I came across the name Gabriel R. Alamo. His photo on the profile was that of an older man. What really got my attention was his display of medals. I couldn't help but notice the World War II campaigns and Korean service medals. This man survived two previous wars. Gabriel Alamo's daughter, Deborah Ann Alamo, posted the memorial for her father on the Virtual Wall site. One can actually feel the love and pride she had for her father, which she delivers in her memorial:

My father was, as were many who gave their lives in Vietnam, an exceptional man. A man of honor and integrity who believed in fighting for his convictions. And this is the lesson of our country's history, that the bravest and the finest are called to give all they have and pay the ultimate price, that all our sons and daughters remain free. Do not ask about the political correctness of the war. Do not try to find the reasons for the battle. Only remember the great courage and integrity they display in choosing to accept the call. Try to emulate their character in your own life, pass their memory down to future generations and save a secret place in your heart to reunite with them often.

Gabriel R. Alamo entered the military before World War II and served with the Eighty-Second Airborne Division during that war. After the war's end, he completed a variety of military courses, finishing the Chemical Corps School in 1950, following which he served in the Korean War. He did overseas tours in occupied Germany and Japan and eventually volunteered for and qualified in the Special Forces. In 1964, Master Sergeant Alamo volunteered for duty in Vietnam, arriving in late spring. He was attached to Detachment A-726, based in Nam Dong, South Vietnam.

The hamlet of Nam Dong lies in a valley just east of the Laotian border and thirty-two miles west of the coastal city of Da Nang. Nam Dong was important for only one reason: it sat astride an infiltration route that connected to the Ho Chi Minh Trail in Laos. A CIDG camp was established in Nam Dong, stiffened by the presence of a twelve-man Special Forces Detachment led by Captain Roger Donlon. Warrant Officer Kevin G. Conway, Royal Australian Army, was attached to the team, and Master Sergeant Gabriel Alamo was the senior enlisted team member.

At about 2:30 a.m. on the morning of July 6, 1964, the camp was taken under attack by two reinforced battalions of Viet Cong, an attack that lasted until well after daybreak. Although the camp's perimeter was breached in several places, the South Vietnamese irregulars and the Special Forces troops held out, but at a very high cost. Most of the local force was killed in action, and so too were Warrant Officer Conway, Sergeant John Houston, and Master Sergeant Alamo.

All the Special Forces men were decorated for heroism: the Medal of Honor to Capt. Donlon, posthumous Distinguished Service Crosses to M.Sgt. Alamo and Sgt. Houston, four Silver Stars (including Warrant Officer Conway) and five Bronze Stars.

Master Sergeant Gabriel R. Alamo's Distinguished Service Cross citation reads as follows:

> *Master Sergeant Gabriel Alamo distinguished himself*
> *by extraordinary heroism in connection with military*
> *operations involving an opposing armed force in the*
> *Republic of Vietnam on 6 July 1964. As a team sergeant,*
> *serving with the US Army Special Forces Detachment A-726*
> *At Camp Nam Dong, Sergeant Gabriel Alamo displayed*
> *bravery, fortitude and perseverance when a reinforced*
> *Viet Cong Battalion suddenly launched a full scale, pre-*
> *dawn attack on the camp. During the violent battle that*
> *ensued, lasting five hours and resulting in heavy*
> *casualties on both sides, he participated with outstand-*
> *ing effectiveness in defending the installation. Upon the*
> *initial onslaught he promptly directed a radio operator to*
> *transmit a message requesting support, and then rushed*
> *into a blazing building to assist in the removal of weapons*
> *and ammunition. Ignoring the burns he received while in*
> *the burning structure, he then ran through a hail of*
> *enemy gunfire to a 60mm mortar position and set the*
> *weapon for firing. As he noticed the enemy attempting*
> *to breach the main gate, he again dashed through a*
> *heavy volume of automatic weapons fire to abort the*
> *hostile action. Although he sustained a serious wound*
> *in this courageous action, he demonstrated superhuman*
> *effort, reached the gate, and prevented entry of enemy*
> *troops. Despite his wound, and intense grenade attack,*
> *he reached the 60mm mortar pit, refused evacuation for*
> *medical treatment, and directed the fire of the 60mm*
> *mortar while simultaneously manning a 57mm recoilless*
> *rifle. Undaunted by the vicious enemy assault, he*
> *remained at his battle position and defended the camp*
> *until mortally wounded by the enemy. Sgt Alamo's*
> *valiant efforts and extraordinary heroic actions are*
> *in the highest traditions of the United States Army*
> *and reflect great credit upon himself and the military*
> *service.*

In 2001, "War Hero's Death Etched in Memory" by John A. Harnes was printed in New Jersey's Coastal Monmouth Bureau. It reads as follows:

On the 37th anniversary of his death in battle, Master Sergeant Gabriel R. Alamo was honored yesterday by his old comrade in arms, retired Colonel Roger H.C. Donlon, the first American to be awarded the Medal of Honor during the Vietnam War.

Already a veteran of WW II and Korea, Alamo was a grizzled 45 year old New Jerseyan affectionately known as "Pop" by his younger colleagues at Nam Dong in the early days of the war.

"He was our leader and inspiration," Donlon told those who gathered at a ceremony at the New Jersey Vietnam Veterans Memorial off the Garden State Parkway. "He was certainly a warrior among warriors."

On July 6, 1964, Donlon was in command of Detachment A-726, 7th Special Forces Group (Airborne), 1st Special Forces, when a reinforced Viet Cong battalion launched a full-scale, pre-dawn attack on the camp.

The ensuing battle lasted five hours and resulted in heavy casualties on both sides. Donlon, then a captain, directed the defense operations in the midst of an enemy barrage of mortar shells, falling grenades and extremely heavy gunfire.

Donlon said the shape of the memorial was similar to that of the mortar pit he and Alamo were literally blown into by an explosion. "To my dying day I will carry the memory of having Pop die in my arms," Donlon said.

The defenders of Nam Dong, outnumbered at least 3 to 1, would become one of the most highly decorated units in Army history.

In addition to Donlon's Medal of Honor, Distinguished Service Crosses, the nation's second-most-sacred awards for military valor, were presented posthumously to Alamo, who hailed from Lyndhurst, and Sergeant John Houston. Four team members were awarded the Silver Star Medal and another five each received the Bronze Star Medal with "V" for valor.

Representing Major General Paul J. Glazar, the states adjutant general, during the ceremony was Colonel Michael Warner, who presented Alamo's son, Michael Sr., with his father's New Jersey Distinguished Service Medal, the state's top military award. After receiving the award, he passed it to his own 16-year-old son, Michael Jr.

Michael Sr. was only 4 when his father died. He reminded onlookers that engraved on the war memorial's walls are the names of people like his father who "gave their lives for their country." He came to the ceremony with his wife, Demy, and children, Michael Jr. and Alyssa, 10, from their home in Alabama.

Michael Sr. said Donlon, now living in Leavenworth, Kansas, recruited him in 1983 and he earned a place in the ranks of the Special Forces and served in the Army for six years.

Donlon said Michael Alamo Sr., now a firefighter/paramedic, is "still battling fires, but this time they are at home."

Donlon quoted a message from Major Michael Davis O'Donnell, who on January 1, 1970, in Dak To, Vietnam, crystallized the sentiments he and other veterans share concerning the loss of men such as Alamo:

"If you are able, save for them a place inside of you and save one backward glance when you are leaving for the places they can no longer go. Be not ashamed to say you loved them, though you may or may not have always. Take what they have left and what they have taught you with their dying and keep it with your own. And in that time when men decide and feel safe to call the war insane, take one moment to embrace those gentle heroes you left behind."

O'Donnell, a helicopter pilot, was killed in action on March 24, 1970, during a rescue attempt.

Gabriel Ralph Alamo's name is located on the Vietnam Memorial Wall, panel 01E, line 057.

Will They Remember

Will they remember us when we are gone,
The battles we fought, the wars we've won?
Will any of this matter to the youth of tomorrow,
The loss of lives, the carnage, the sorrow?

Will they remember the reason we fought,
The freedom provided, the democracy we brought?
Or will this all be passed off as an old cliché
A patriotic rhetoric from their grandparent's day?

Will they remember as a hearse rolls by,
With a flag-draped casket resting inside,
To show gratitude and respect, if only in thought,
For the hero within and the freedom he's brought?

Will they remember the spine-tingling sound
As a bugle blows "taps" at the burial ground?
Will they remember to honor the military man
Regardless of their political stand?

Will they remember the sacrifice
And that freedom comes at a very steep price?
A bill that was started so long ago,
And is still being paid by many they will never know.

M.Sgt. Billy F. Dial
US Marine Corp

WILLIAM KAPENA ALAMEDA

    I knew a kid in high school named Bill Alameda. When I saw William Alameda's name on the Virtual Wall website, I had to check it out to see if he was the same kid I went to high school with. Not the same Alameda, but nevertheless an intriguing story comes out of a memorial posted by William Kapena Alameda's daughter, Sarah Michel.

    I had the pleasure of meeting the wonderful Sarah Michel in San Diego. When I asked her if I could include her story in my book, she was extremely excited about sharing with me her father's story and of her journey of self-discovery. And for that, Sarah, I thank you.

    Fire Support Base Rita, located near the Cambodian border in the Fishhook area, had been established to block NVA infiltration from Cambodia into South Vietnam. It was occupied by elements of B Company, First

Battalion, Twenty-Sixth Infantry, B Troop, First Squadron, Fourth Calvary, B Battery, First Battalion, Fifth Artillery and C Battery, Eighth Battalion, Sixth Artillery.

Just after 0300 on the morning of November 1, 1968, FSB Rita came under attack by North Vietnamese Army units. At the outset, the base was subjected to heavy mortar, artillery, and RPG attack, followed by a "human wave" assault against the northwestern defensive perimeter. Sappers and enemy infantry penetrated the perimeter, resulting in fighting within the northwestern section of FSB Rita. The First Battalion, Fifth Artillery commanding officer, Lieutenant-Colonel Charles C. Rogers, rallied his men and beat back the initial assault. A second massed assault followed, and again Lt. Col. Rogers led a successful defense. All six 105 howitzers were soon under attack. Corporal William Alameda was manning one of those howitzers. He was the only man standing. Cpl. Alameda initiated direct howitzer fire at the assailants. Lt. Col. Rogers and 1st Lt. Callahan came to Alameda's position in order to help beehive the sappers directly. A mortar round landed at the left wheel, wounding Cpl. Alameda, Lt. Col. Rogers, and 1st Lt. Callahan. Cpl. Alameda continued firing upon the enemy until he was mortally wounded by a recoilless rifle. As dawn broke, a third massed attack was launched. Rogers, now with four serious wounds, no longer was able to physically lead his men but continued to direct the defense, and once again, the NVA were repulsed. The battle continued until about 0800, when increasing air support forced the NVA to break off the attack and retreat across the border to sanctuary in Cambodia.

Lieutenant-Colonel Rogers was awarded the Medal of Honor for his actions during Operation Fishhook. Corporal William Alameda was awarded the Bronze Star Medal with combat V device posthumously.

Corporal William K. Alameda's Bronze Star Citation reads as follows:

> *For heroism not involving participation in aerial flight, in connection with military operations against a hostile force in the Republic of Vietnam. On 1 November, 1968, Corporal Alameda was serving as a section chief with his battery located at a fire support base in enemy infested territory. When the friendly position was subjected to intense hostile mortar fire and a subsequent ground assault, Corporal Alameda immediately rushed to his gun emplacement. As incoming rounds impacted all around, he began firing an effective counter mortar program at the insurgent's positions. The advancing Viet Cong soon approached one sector of the perimeter and the*

*American defenses were in danger of being overrun.
Corporal Alameda reacted quickly to the hazardous
situation, and initiated direct howitzer fire at the
assailants. With complete disregard for his personal
safety, he maintained his open, forward position and
continued his devastating fire on the hostile force
until he was mortally wounded by a recoilless rifle
round. The selfless courage and staunch determination
of Corporal Alameda while braving intense enemy fire
were instrumental in limiting casualties among his
comrades, and significantly contributed to the
successful defense of the friendly position. Corporal
Alameda's outstanding display of aggressiveness,
devotion to duty, and personal bravery is in keeping
with the finest traditions of the military service and
reflects great credit upon himself, the 1st Infantry
Division, and the United States Army.
By direction of the President.*

Before Cpl. Alameda died, he managed to give another soldier a picture of his fiancée. He asked the soldier to find her and give her the picture. "Tell her I love her and am sorry that I won't be there for her and the baby." The soldier found Mai Tran in the nearby village of Loc Ninh and, after giving her the picture, told her that William Alameda died bravely in a firefight a few days earlier. Mai Tran was not surprised. William had never gone three days without seeing her. She heard the sound of battle in the distant area of the artillery base. She sensed that William was dead. The pain finally hit Mai Tran in the stomach, or perhaps it was the unborn baby beginning to kick inside her.

Mai Tran washed clothes for the soldiers at the Army outpost near Loc Ninh. The pay was good per Vietnam standards. She needed to stay busy and concentrate on the well-being of her soon-to-be-born baby. She would lie in her bed at night and hold her stomach and feel the baby move inside her. She prayed that the war would end soon so she could raise her new child without worry. She knew that the baby would fill a void in her life. She missed William terribly. As the baby moved inside her womb, she would tell the unborn baby stories about her and William. She told the baby how much she loved William because he always made her laugh. When they first met, William hired a translator so they could communicate. After a while, she learned enough English and William learned enough Vietnamese that they could spend time alone without the translator. She told the unborn child about how William made funny music with a funny little guitar. He was being silly hopping around on one leg, playing that funny little guitar.

For the next three months, Mai Tran continued her ritual of entertaining the unborn child with stories of its father. On February 1, 1969, Mai Tran gave birth to a girl. She named the baby My Traing. Baby My was extremely beautiful. So peaceful in her sleep, Mai observed, yet in a place without peace. She could see William in baby My's face. She also knew that the Viet Cong would be equally observant. There was the constant fear of what the Viet Cong would do to her or her baby if or when they would return to her village. Even with the American forces nearby, her daily life was filled with fear. There were no signs of the war coming to an end. The war appeared to be escalating with the constant infiltration of the NVA and Viet Cong in the Tay Ninh Province. Mai Tran reasoned that the safest thing she could do for her daughter and for herself is to send My Traing to an orphanage.

My Traing was quickly adopted by a young couple from Michigan. Her adoptive parents named her Sarah Michel. Until she was sixteen, Sarah had big question marks for her biological parents. She also thought she was half African American. But one day, her adoptive parents got a call from their adoption agency. Sarah's mother, Mai Tran, was looking for her daughter.

Their first conversation, which was over the phone, consisted of little more than crying. They met a few months later, and Sarah learned she had three half siblings, two by a Vietnamese father and one by an American doctor.

When Sarah got older, she gradually gained interest in her father. Who was he? she would ask her mother. What did he like to do? What did he look like? Many times, Sarah's mother clammed up at the questioning. But sometimes she would talk about him—his dashing good looks, his sweet lilting voice, and his knack for music.

Sarah's mother did not know where William Alameda was from or whether he had family. Finally, Sarah stopped asking about her father. She gave up on the search. But her fiancé, Johan Oeyen, did not. He was intent on finding her father and, for more than two years, searched military websites and databases for any Alan, Allen, or William he could find. He found nothing.

The breakthrough came all at once—and purely by mistake. For years, Sarah's mother had been saying Alameda's middle name was something like "Alan." It wasn't always clear because of the language barrier between mother and daughter. At the dinner table one day, Oeyen spelled the name out and asked, "Like this?" "No," Sarah's mother said. It was A-L-A-M. At first, Oeyen thought the name was Middle Eastern. Then he went to an Internet listing of those whose names are on the Vietnam Veterans Memorial Wall in Washington, DC. When he typed in the four letters, three names came up: two Alamos and one Alameda.

When Sarah saw her father's name, she said, "William Alameda, that's my dad. I just had a feeling. I knew it instantly." She had found the man who had fallen in love with her mother and died before she was born.

They found out that William Alameda had been in Vietnam about the time Sarah was conceived and was based in Tay Ninh, where Mai Tran had worked and where My Traing was born.

Immediately, Oeyen began calling members of the Alameda family living in Hawaii. One of the first to receive a call was Gordon Alameda, one of William Alameda's brothers. "I told him, 'There's a lot of Alamedas on this island. You must have the wrong Alameda," Gordon Alameda said. Gordon Alameda had never heard of his brother William having a child or even a girlfriend while in Vietnam.

But a few phone calls later, there could be no mistaking Sarah's lineage. "Every time she called, I'd say, 'Eh, she sounds like Auntie Leo," Gordon said. Sarah and the Alameda family began swapping pictures and were soon convinced that Sarah was a relative.

A DNA test completed in December 2005 confirmed William Alameda was Sarah's father. Now, Sarah is learning everything she can about the father she never knew. She also has a new family, and she is quickly learning about each family member with enthusiasm.

In January 2006, Sarah and Oeyen flew to Hawaii to meet her new family. Twenty of her uncles, aunts, and cousins greeted them at the airport. After only two days in Hawaii, Sarah said that it already feels like home.

The family gathered for a picnic at Makapu'u. They were all excited about welcoming Sarah to the Alameda family. "I feel complete now," said Sarah, surrounded by her new family. "I had this longing for my father, and now I feel complete."

Alfred Alameda, another brother of William, said he never needed any convincing, DNA test or otherwise, that Sarah was indeed his niece. "There wasn't a doubt in my mind," he said.

In 1934, George and Edna Alameda wed on the island of Oahu. They had eleven children. Seven boys and four girls: Edna (named after her mother), seventy-two; George (Uncle Bully), seventy-one; Henri (Uncle Dundang), sixty-nine; Sammy, sixty-eight; Alice, sixty-five; William (Billy Boy), killed in action, 1968, in Vietnam; Joe, sixty, passed away in 1997; Lena (Auntie Tita), fifty-eight, passed away in 1997; Leona (Auntie Leo), fifty-five; Alfred (Uncle Choppers), fifty-three; and Gordon (Uncle Kanani), fifty-nine.

The family shared many stories with Sarah about her dad. His passion for music. He was quite the ukulele player and often sang at family gatherings. He also enjoyed making people laugh. Often, unintentionally. Wilfred, William's cousin and best friend growing up, remembers:

I was about twelve, and so was Billy Boy. Joey, his brother, joined us for a fishing trip. After several hours of not catching anything, we started walking back home. Billy Boy was carrying his pole over his shoulder. Bait was still on the hook, and the line was dangling freely. While horseplaying around during the walk, the line swung over and caught Joey in the mouth. The barbed hook was lodged in Joey's lip and the boys couldn't get the hook out. Billy Boy fulfilled his promise by not coming home without hooking the biggest fish. A man passing by in a truck saw the situation and stopped to help. He was a friendly Japanese fellow who got his knife out and cut the line and the hook. Joey was relieved, but I think Billy Boy was a little disappointed that he didn't get to show his big fish to Mom and Dad.

The family took Sarah and Oeyen to visit her dad's grave at the National Memorial Cemetery of the Pacific at Punchbowl. Tears were plentiful. With every hug from uncles and aunts was a true sense of her father's presence. William Kapena Alameda was looking down at Sarah, and she could feel a love that she had never experienced. It was a love that could only be shared by a father and daughter. She could hear the ukulele making sweet music.

William Kapena Alameda's name is located on the Vietnam Memorial Wall, panel 40W, line 70.

If I Die Before You Wake

If I die before you wake, I pray that you will not forsake
The sacrifice made in freedom's name
By those who cannot wake again.

And if I die before you wake
I pray that with your life you make
A thing of beauty from the ash,
The sacrifice of those who've passed.

Oh, if I die before you wake
It's only death, the common fate
That comes to all, to some too soon
But come it did and now I'm gone.

No tears you cry will call me home
Nor questions why, empty my tomb
Not want of answers nor roll of drums
Not bugle calls or poet's songs.

No deed or word or hope or prayer
Shall call me to stand beside you there.
In death I lay, in death I've gone
But you've the chance to carry on.

Don't let my deeds have been in vain
Don't with my death accede to pain
But rise anew, strive to attain
A better world in my good name.

Oh, if I die before you wake
With your life a goodness make
Dust off the ash, greatness attain
For I can never rise again.

In death I lay, in death I've gone
Yours is the task to carry on
To do with your life the beautiful things
That only life to mankind brings.

If I die before you wake.

Sgt. Eric Schrumph
US Marine Corps

Timothy Joseph Rizzardini

I would like to know more about Tim Rizzardini's life. After reading the following story in the June 2007 issue of *Vietnam* magazine, I tried to locate relatives and men that served with Timothy Rizzardini. My search hit a dead end. However, I was fortunate in locating George J. Hawkins, the author. I was unable to find a photo of Mr. Rizzardini. I would like to express my gratitude to Mr. Hawkins for allowing me to put his story, "Horseman, Pass By," in my book. *Vietnam* magazine also deserves a big thank you.

> *The first time I met Goodbody was on a high, mist shrouded mountaintop in Hiep Duc Valley, southwest of Da Nang. It was 1968, and we were both in the 196th Light Infantry Brigade. A small landing zone (LZ) had been slashed in a level spot near the top of the mountain. The chopper I was on circled yellow smoke marking the LZ, then swooped down over some thick bamboo and hovered noisily a few feet off the ground while I jumped off.*
>
> *I crouched low beneath the whirling chopper blade and scrambled off to the side of the LZ where two stubble-bearded grunts sat reading paperbacks. I dropped my pack and stood there feeling a bit awkward as I looked around watching the chopper being unloaded and listening to the high-pitched whine of the engine.*
>
> *Putting their books away, both grunts motioned for me to join them at the edge of the LZ. When the chopper finally took off, we shook hands and introduced ourselves. The tall lanky guy with black curly hair sitting on a mud-covered helmet told me his name was Spider. His buddy, with a thick, drooping handlebar mustache, introduced himself as Goodbody. Later that day when I was assigned to their squad, I learned that Goodbody was his nickname. I don't recall anyone ever calling him by his real name.*

As we sat talking in the tall green elephant grass, I noticed that Goodbody was reading Eric Hoffer's The True Believer. *I had finished the book a short time before arriving in country, so we launched into a discussion that evolved into an exchange of opinions on subjects ranging from literature to beer. I also learned that Goodbody graduated from college, like me, not long before being drafted into the Army. Although he majored in history and political science, he had developed a passion for literature, so when he graduated he had more credits in English than in his major. This mirrored my own academic history.*

In the months that followed, we became squad members and close friends. Whenever we stopped, whether for a smoke break or to dig a foxhole for a night laager position or to heat up a can of C-rations, we would talk about literature, women, and especially what we planned to do when we got back to "The World." That was our escape, our way of blotting out the terrible reality we were caught up in. Once, I gave Goodbody a book of Irish short stories—a tattered old paperback I'd bought in Seattle shortly before our battalion was sent to Vietnam. A few of James Joyce's stories were included in the anthology. We both agreed that "Araby" was one of his best. One of the few things we disagreed about was the cryptic passage by William Butler Yeats at the beginning of the short story anthology. We never could come to terms with the Yeats passage (an epitaph he wrote for himself):

> *Cast a cold eye*
> *On life, on death.*
> *Horseman, pass by!*

Goodbody believed the horseman was a symbol of death: no emotions were involved—the horseman simply collected his bounty. I thought Yeats was telling us to live life and not concern ourselves with death. As time passed, we came closer to a more agreeable interpretation, but we were never completely satisfied.

Goodbody was especially fond of Eugene O'Neil's gripping play Long Day's Journey Into Night. *He planned to do some writing when he got out of Vietnam and out of the Army.*

We got separated after spending five months in the same squad, but occasionally we would run into each other on fire support bases. We always managed to trade paperbacks, scrounge up a few beers and have a talk.

Once we met north of Hue, just after Goodbody had been through some hairy action there. He told me his company was making contact with NVA regulars every day. I gave him a copy of Robert Frost's poems

I'd been carrying in my pack for a month. He showed me a cigarette lighter he'd bought in Thailand while on R&R. It had the Yeats passage inscribed on it. I pulled my new lighter from my fatigues with the same passage engraved on it. We laughed and drank our warm beer. He told me his company was going back to Que Son Valley, an NVA stronghold. Goodbody had been through hell there before, and never wanted to return. When we parted, he put the book of poems in the leg pocket of his jungle fatigues and slipped his lighter into his jacket pocket along with his cigarettes.

Soon afterward, he was walking point on Hill 205. It was a dark, moonless night. NVA were on top of the hill waiting. Goodbody walked into a thousand muzzle flashes. It was chaos. It was instant death for him and another fine soldier. Then it was over. They had to leave Goodbody on the hill for a night and a day.

Two days after the firefight, I got on a chopper at LZ West. It was transporting two dead soldiers back to graves registration in Da Nang. Both bodies were wrapped in muddy, bloodstained ponchos. There was a thick stench in the chopper even though plenty of air rushed in the open sides. Halfway through the flight, the wind blew part of a poncho off the face of one of the dead soldiers. It was Goodbody. I turned away and stared down at the blurred green-and-brown checkerboard patterns of the rice paddies below. All I could think of was the line from Yeats, "Horseman, pass by!"

Thirty years later, Memorial Day weekend 1998, I was heading down California's highway 101 south of Santa Cruz, my current home. Off to my right was the Pacific Ocean. I was driving 360 miles to Ridgecrest, California, a small town in the Mojave Desert, to visit Goodbody's grave. Up until a few weeks prior, I hadn't even known his real name.

In the journal I kept during my tour of duty in Vietnam, I had noted his name as Tim R. Why did I wait almost 30 years to sleuth out his real name and hometown? I have no excuse, but I wasn't the most stable person on my return to The World. I moved a lot, changed jobs often, got married and divorced. I thought of him often in the years after my discharge from the Army. I guessed that my chances of finding him were good; at least I knew he was from California.

The years rolled by. In the mid-'90s, a buddy from Vietnam, Bill Hankins, from Tucker, Arkansas, telephoned out of the blue. Somehow he had found me over the internet. Bill, Goodbody and I had been in the same company in Vietnam. The subject of Goodbody eased its way into our conversation. I may have promised Bill I would start my search, if for no other reason than to honor Goodbody by visiting his grave and close the loop that had remained open for so many years. Perhaps I would meet with his parents, tell them something they already knew, something like: "Your son was one of the finest people I ever knew, a true patriot, a hero who laid down his life for his brothers in arms. Me, I was just a friend of his, I was lucky, I got to come home. I'm alive."

Over time, sure enough I found Goodbody's real name on one of the websites inspired by the Vietnam Veteran's Memorial. Copious tears flowed as I read the listing:

Timothy Joseph Razzardini, SP4, Army, Selective Service, 196th Light Infantry Brigade, Male, Born on October 22, 1944. His tour of duty began December 3, 1967, casualty was on May 18, 1968 in Quang Tin, South Vietnam, hostile ground casualty, multiple fragmentation wounds. Body was recovered. Religion, Roman Catholic.

So here I was on a pilgrimage to Goodbody's grave in the desert town of Ridgecrest, population 24,000 and change. It was the least I could do. I was driving my 1974 Plymouth Duster with 128,000 miles on the odometer. The front end was kind of squirrelly, the brake pads chattered on steep downhills, and the 318 V-8 guzzled oil. Being the third owner, I was fairly certain everything from the radiator cap to the rear end was original. If the Duster broke down along the way and I couldn't fix it, I'd sell it to the nearest junkyard and hitchhike or catch a bus. One way or another, I would get there.

Late that day, the Duster cruised into Ridgecrest, where I found an inexpensive motel and rented a room. At 6 p.m. the temperature was hovering around 102 degrees. Next morning, I drove to the small cemetery on the outskirts of town. There could not have been more than a thousand graves. Already, VFW volunteers were in the process of marking all the veteran's graves with small U.S. flags. I checked every grave with a flag on it, but could not find Goodbody's. I panicked: Maybe I was in the wrong town. Could there be more than one Ridgecrest in the state of California? Maybe he was buried in a military cemetery, or maybe I had dreamed up this whole thing. Seeing my bewilderment, one of the volunteers stopped to ask if he could be of any help. I explained that I was looking for the grave of Timothy Rizzardini, killed in Vietnam, 1968. "Oh yes, right this way," he said, leading me straight to Goodbody's gravesite. The gravestone read "Timothy J. Rizzardini, 1944-1968." There was no mention of the Army or Vietnam.

The next morning, on Memorial Day, an honor guard and members of the local VFW post conducted a graveside ceremony, as they do every year, to honor all war dead. Paying my respects to Goodbody, I felt a trace of guilt for having survived while he paid the ultimate price. As I stared down at the gravestone, my only thought was "Horseman, pass by."

Timothy Joseph Razzardini's name is located on the Vietnam Memorial Wall, panel 62E, line 22.

PAUL FREDERICK COBB

My best friend Nathaniel Holmes III, whom I have known for forty years, recently invited me to attend the reunion of Alpha Company, First Battalion, Seventh Marines. Since he has attended my reunions, I thought it only fair to take him up on his offer. At his reunion in San Antonio, Texas, many of us Marines sat around a table telling war stories. I shared with them my new project, which happens to be this book, and I also shared with them some bits and pieces about some of the men I am writing about. Nat suggested that I should consider including their platoon commander who died heroically while in Vietnam. All the other old warriors sitting at the table agreed enthusiastically.

I would like to thank Nat Holmes and the men of 1/7 for turning me on to the Paul Cobb story. I would also like to thank Paul Cobb Jr. for providing me with newspaper clippings and numerous articles about his father.

On November 23, 1996, a college football game took place at Blacksburg, Virginia. The two opposing teams were Virginia Tech and West Virginia. There was a sellout crowd as usual between these two rivals. There was a halftime ceremony honoring one of Virginia Techs former students, Paul Frederick Cobb. A $75,000 scholarship was announced in his name.

Quite often the fans will shrug off the halftime activities and go about their normal routine and scramble to beat the long lines to the restrooms or to grab a popcorn and soft drink. Or simply to yak it up with old friends. The game, after all, is what brought them there in the first place.

Well, that was one break between blocking and tackling that deserved attention. Freddie Cobb, Tech class of '66, was special. Longtime Hokies fans might have difficulty remembering him.

A native of Suffolk, Virginia, Cobb was an outstanding quarterback at Woodrow Wilson High in Portsmouth. In his senior season, he received numerous offers to play college football. Cobb opted instead to attend Fork Union Military Academy for the 1961 and 1962 sessions, following in the footsteps of his father (William Chester Cobb III, class of 1931).

And unlike most halftimes, a majority of the audience stayed in their seats through the stoppage of play. Tech Athletic Director Dave Blaine said that there probably wasn't more than ten bags of popcorn sold. The ceremony for Cobb, who was well liked during his time at Tech, included performances from university groups and the Marine Corp's Silent Drill Team. There were few dry eyes in the stadium.

Why would there be a scholarship announced in his name? Cobb seldom got on the field during his five seasons as a quarterback/defensive back. A drop-back quarterback with a strong arm, Cobb measured his time in minutes for a team that featured a rollout offense. By his admission, Cobb was slow afoot. Freddie Cobb walked in the shadow of heroes. He never made a play to win the big game. He logged only about twenty minutes total playing time. The cheers were always for someone else.

Following his time at Fork Union, Freddie chose Virginia Tech. He did not realize it at the time, but his drop-back style did not fit into coach Jerry Claiborne's rollout system at Tech. Cobb never became a first team player for the Hokies on teams from 1964 to 1966.

He did not, however, let that dampen his enthusiasm for Virginia Tech. "I came here for an education first," he told a newsman later. "Besides, this is where I met my wife, Bonnie. I have no regrets at all."

Claiborne later described Cobb as one of his favorite players and said, "Even though he knew he probably would not play in the games, he came to practice with great enthusiasm and gave 100 percent on every play. His spirit rubbed off on all those around him. Cobb endeared himself to me and to his teammates with his hustling attitude."

During practice a squad, called the scout team, would function as the opposing team that Tech would play that week. Cobb was usually the quarterback for this group and would call the plays that the opposition's quarterback was likely to use.

Cobb's presence was a big factor in the success of Tech's defense at that time. "He was one of those unsung heroes that just got the team ready each week," said Peter Dawyot, who was a defensive tackle for Tech.

In the final weeks of his collegiate career, Cobb insisted he had no regrets going to Tech. "When I started playing football, I learned that slogan. You know, the one that goes, 'A winner never quits and a quitter never wins.' I believed it. I still believe it," he said in an article that appeared in the *Richmond Times-Dispatch*. "I've followed that saying all my life. When I get down in the dumps, I remember it. Look! In wartime, what if they (soldiers, sailors, Marines) would quit? Where would we be now?"

Freddie was talking about the Vietnam War. He had just enlisted in the United States Marine Corps' Officer Candidates School, volunteering for the infantry. With a degree in business administration in December 1966, Cobb was off to Quantico, Virginia.

Freddie Cobb finally got to play a lot of football when he was in training at the Marine base at Quantico. In the fall of 1967, playing drop-back quarterback for the Quantico team that played other service bases and selected college teams like William and Mary, Cobb so impressed the Baltimore Colts that they offered him a tryout. What's more, if he would agree to it, they said they could fix it so he would not have to go to Vietnam. Freddie's response was pretty quick. "I've signed a contract. I'm going to pull duty. If you guys want to talk to me when I get back . . ."

Cal Esleeck, a classmate of Cobb's at Virginia Tech and later a Marine Corps officer beside him, recalls a special night with Cobb in a Marine barracks at Quantico:

> There were about 10 or 12 of us there. Freddie came in and told me Bonnie was pregnant. He was very happy about that. Then all of a sudden, Freddie Cobb, who could go all day and only say about six words, suddenly became very talkative. He talked to the group about attitude, how we must learn our lessons well, and take a positive approach to everything. Everyone in that room listened, and they walked away with a different outlook on life.

We didn't have the sense to know it at the time, but we had just gotten a lesson in leadership. It was something I will never forget.

Freddie met Bonnie during the summer of 1965. Mutual friends had invited them for a leisurely afternoon drive to Smith Mountain Lake. Bonnie was going steady with a boy from Georgetown University at the time. Freddie agreed to go on the drive but made it perfectly clear that he wasn't interested in any kind of relationship. "We really hit it off," Bonnie said, "but due to my college relationship, did not see each other again that summer." Bonnie broke up with the boy from Georgetown later that summer. Freddie was playing ball that fall. Arrangements were made by their mutual friends to double-date after a game. That was all it took, and by Christmas of 1965, they were engaged. Freddie and Bonnie were married the following June.

Bonnie remembers:

> *I was attracted initially to Freddie by his looks, his personality, his character, and his faith. Not in that order of importance, but in that order I met and was attracted to him. On that summer day that we met, he said, "I don't intend to marry for a long time because I want to go into the Marine Corps and will likely go overseas. I don't want to bring a wife into that risk." He shortly changed his mind about marriage but not his desire to be a Marine.*
>
> *Freddie's love for Jesus Christ was of upmost importance to him. On his desk in Vietnam, he kept out the verse from the New Testament, Philippians 4:13: "I can do all things through Christ who strengthens me." After his death, one of the most poignant letters I received was from the battalion chaplain who had become friends with Freddie. Chaplain Vincent Krulak told of how he and Freddie shared times talking of their faith and their wives and family. Freddie would often fill in for the chaplain in leading worship services when the chaplain was away.*
>
> *Freddie was so excited about becoming a father. I know it was hard on him to be away when Paul was born, and he was so excited to talk with me about him after his birth and to receive pictures of his new son.*
>
> *Some years later, after I had remarried, my mother had related something Freddie had said to her. In talking about friends and his years at Virginia Tech, he said, "A teammate and friend I admire the most is Dave Gillespie." If those who have gone before us to heaven know what goes on in our lives (and I believe that the Bible indicates that they do), I am sure that Freddie smiled to see Dave become Paul's daddy in his absence.*

Second Lieutenant Paul Frederick Cobb had shipped out to Vietnam in January 1968. He was assigned as second platoon commander with Alpha Company, First Battalion, Seventh Marine Regiment, First Marine Division. Green, inexperienced butter bars, as second lieutenants were often called, were seldom welcomed with open arms. By many grizzled grunts, they were considered a nuisance and a great threat to their survival. 2nd Lt. Cobb was an exception. He relied on his warriors who survived many firefights. The transition from being an observer to a leader was quick as was the confidence of his Marines.

Staff Sergeant Lawrence Peterson was Cobb's platoon sergeant.

> *I remember in early May of '68, Lt. Cobb was sitting on an ammo bunker reading his mail. I took a seat next to him to read my mail. The lieutenant was all smiles. He showed me some pictures of his new son, Paul Jr. I said to him in a joking manner, "You sure do look like him, sir." He tried to correct me and said, "No, sergeant, he looks like me." To which I told him, "No, sir, you look just like that little baby. Are you sure he's not your little brother?" I was referring to his baby-face looks, which he accepted without argument. He told me that he couldn't wait to go on R & R in Hawaii to see his wife, Bonnie, and little Paul. "I want to hug my wife, and I want to hug my new son. I can't wait to hold my son in my arms," he said.*

During Operation Allen Brook in the Quang Nam Province, Lieutenant Cobb's platoon was assigned the mission of reinforcing an adjacent unit, which was heavily engaged with a well-entrenched enemy force and had sustained numerous casualties. The official report reads:

> *Under intense fire, Lt Cobb led his men to a position behind the most heavily engaged element of the besieged company where he prepared to continue the attack against the enemy. In order that the pinned-down Marines could evacuate their casualties from the fire-swept area, he established a base of fire utilizing small arms and M-79 grenade launcher fire and began maneuvering his unit across the hazardous terrain. Forced to crawl forward toward the hostile emplacements due to the heavy volume of enemy's automatic weapons, machine guns, B-40 rocket and mortar fire, he ignored the fire striking around him, as he shouted directions and encouragement to his men. As he approached to within 20 meters of the enemy's positions, he was wounded by hostile fire; however, he aggressively led his men in hand-to-hand combat.*

*While maneuvering forward with his men, he was mortally wounded
by the enemy fire. His courageous leadership during the ensuing assaults
inspired his men to continue to advance and overwhelm the enemy to the
point of defeat. By his bold determination and unwavering and selfless
dedication to duty, Lieutenant Cobb upheld the highest traditions of the
Marine Corps and the United States Naval Service. He gallantly gave
his life for his country.*

Lt. Paul Frederick Cobb was posthumously awarded the Navy Cross, the
military's second highest honor.

Freddie Cobb's memory is still very much alive today. There are awards in
his name at all the schools he attended, where recipients are recognized not
only for their skill in sports but their character as well. Meanwhile, Freddie's
younger brother, Bobby Cobb, director of development at Fork Union Military
Academy and a freshman there when Freddie was killed, was informed that
Virginia Tech has established an endowed scholarship in Freddie's name.
Bobby hopes that the recipient of the scholarship will be a Fork Union cadet.

For those who knew Freddie, the way he lived his life and the way he died
were one and the same. That same determination, which made him a standout
at Fork Union Military Academy and Virginia Tech, allowed him to lead his
men to victory on the battlefield.

Paul Frederick Cobb's name is located on the Vietnam Memorial Wall, panel
61E, line 007.

A Shadow on the Wall

It was 2:00 a.m. in the morning, when he came upon the Wall,
A dark black V of granite, it stands not very tall.

The timing was premeditated, he had to be alone,
For its very hard to hear, a voice that's etched in stone.

He paced those wings of black, looking for a friend,
And reflect upon a moment in time, to a place they had once been.

Then the panel suddenly appeared, and the voice was once again heard,
A long-lost friend had been found, among the whisper of his word.

In the silence of the night, it echoed from the Wall,
"You can let it go now, and thanks for coming to call."

And then he moved away, the silhouetted wall began to fade,
But looking back, he noticed—his shadow—it had stayed.

Michael "Tiny" Readinger

VINCENT ROBERT CAPODANNO

During the Vietnam War, 240 men received the nation's highest military award, the Medal of Honor. Of those 240 brave men, 149 received the Medal of Honor posthumously, including Vincent Capodanno.

Vincent Capodanno grew up in the thirties and forties in a large Italian American family on Staten Island, New York, the youngest of nine children. His was a typical education of an ordinary American of his time. He worked on Wall Street before deciding to become a priest. He responded to the call of his vocation and joined the Maryknoll missionary order. Upon ordination in 1958, he served in Taiwan and later in Hong Kong. His life might well have ended in the quiet dedication required of missionary life in faraway lands. However, in the mid-'60s, the direction of his life abruptly changed when he volunteered to serve as a Navy/Marine Corps chaplain in Vietnam.

James Capodanno, the chaplain's eldest surviving brother and a World War II Marine veteran, recalls: "We were poor growing up during the Depression. I think Vincent learned from our family's experiences of being poor. It moved him to dedicate his life to service and making sure that no one he met felt they were in need and alone."

In his new assignment as a Navy/Marine chaplain, Fr. Capodanno found a parish among the "needy." He sought the lonely Marines, the grunts who were exposed to death, suffering, and sacrifice. He felt a compelling desire to be with these forgotten parishioners in their greatest hours of need. On April 30, 1966, Fr. Capodanno began a sixteen-month tour with the Seventh and Fifth Marine Regiments where he became the "best-known and sought-after chaplain in the Marine Corps." "What set Father Vincent apart was the way he lived his ministry with the Marines," writes Father Daniel Mode. "He was not a religious leader who did his job and then returned to the comfort of his own circle. He lived as a grunt Marine. Wherever they went, he went. Whatever burdens they had to carry, he shared the load. No problem was too large or too small to take to Father Vincent—he was available to them day and night." The Marines responded to his devotion, and soon he became affectionately known to his Marines as the Grunt Padre.

Thus began an active life of dedication and service that went beyond the call of duty. He became a true father to young boys on the frontlines. He was "out there" with his men where he lived, ate, and slept as they did. To the young Marines thrust into the terrifying reality of battle, he was always available in his tent where anyone could drop in for comfort and guidance. He shared his salary, rations, and cigarettes with anyone in need. He could always be counted upon for a cold soda or a book from his reading library. When Christmas came around and the young grunts felt forgotten, Fr. Vincent saw to it that no Marine was without gifts, which he obtained through a relentless campaign from friends and organizations all over the world. More importantly, he heard confessions for hours on end, instructed converts, and administered the sacraments. His granting of general absolution before battle unburdened the consciences of the Marines and instilled in them to fight with courage. His mere presence in a unit was enough to lift the morale of all on patrol. When men died, he was at their side so they would not die alone. He gave them last rites, encouraging them to repent and persevere. In addition, he wrote countless letters of personal condolence to parents of wounded and dead Marines and offered solid grounding and hope to fellow Marines who lost friends. When the pseudo-peace movement began to oppose the war, Fr. Vincent raised the spirits of demoralized Marines in the field. He encouraged his men to oppose that same brutal communist system, which still oppresses Vietnam today.

However, it was in battle where Fr. Capodanno excelled and inspired. He would find out from friends in military intelligence which unit was most likely to encounter the heaviest enemy contact and volunteer for those assignments. Marines would find him walking dangerous perimeters and keeping company with them in distant jungle outposts. The Grunt Padre could be seen leaping out of a helicopter in the midst of battle. He would care for the wounded, bless troops, and give communion to Catholics, before taking off for another battle zone. Despite the prosaic conditions of battle and an ecumenical chaplain corps, nothing could deviate him from his burning desire to give everything in the service of God, the church, and his men.

The September 1967 elections in South Vietnam meant increased military action by the North Vietnamese Army in efforts to disrupt the voting process. The routine "search and destroy" operation known as Operation Swift began in the early hours of September 4, 1967. It quickly turned into a scene of vicious fighting and inspiring heroism. As companies Bravo and Delta, 1/5 were outnumbered and overwhelmed by 2,500 NVA, the chaplain arrived with the Marines of companies Kilo and Mike to provide much needed reinforcements.

So intense was the ground fire that their helicopters were forced to land some distance away from their intended destination. The Fifth Marines found themselves in dire straits. Although wounded three times in the course of the battle, Fr. Capodanno refused medical evacuation.

Throughout the devastating fighting that ensued, Chaplain Capodanno carried wounded Marines and repeatedly moved back and forth through enemy fire. Like a ray of hope in the midst of the storm, he administered last rites to dying Marines and assisted the wounded with words of comfort. Corporal Ray Harton was among them, shot in the arm, bleeding and fallen to the ground. The fear that grips a man in such a situation is impossible to describe.

Suddenly Ray felt someone touch him. It was Father Vincent. He was on his knees, and amidst the chaos of enemy fire and the cries of the wounded, his manner remained quiet and comforting. He radiated the peace of Christ in a place as far removed from that peace. "For one moment," recalls Corporal Harton, "there was no pain, no screaming, no war."

All the while Chaplain Capodanno was himself badly wounded by shrapnel lodged in his right arm, hand, and leg. Not only did he refuse medical attention, his mission to bring the sacraments to the wounded Marines and offer the comforting love of Christ during their dying moments continued relentlessly. So powerful was the desire to bring the peace of Christ that passes all understanding to those Marines in that place. Putting his left arm under Ray's head, he spoke comforting and cherished words: "God is here with us, Marine, and help is on the way." Then he blessed the wounded Marine with his left hand, having lost most of his own bandaged and bleeding right hand.

With enemy fire quickly enclosing them on all sides, several more men fell to the ground. Capodanno noticed corpsman Armando "Doc" Leal tending wounded Marines across the knoll in an enemy machine-gun's direct line of fire. The wounded chaplain sprinted toward the position, and as the machine-gun opened up, he shielded the corpsman and a cluster of Marines by placing his body between them and the hostile fire. With twenty-seven bullet wounds in his back, neck, and head, the Grunt Padre fell in battle, serving his men to the end. All over Vietnam, the Marines mourned their Padre.

The same self-emptying love of Christ on the cross now inspired Father Capodanno's selfless actions for the souls of wounded Marines. The scorching jungle battlefield was his Calvary.

The memory of Father Vincent Capodanno's sacrifice went beyond his death. His actions on the field of battle that day earned him the nation's highest honor, the Congressional Medal of Honor. Despite the pacifist objections of seventy-three Maryknoll priests, brothers, and seminarians, the Navy commissioned a destroyer escort in 1973: the USS *Capodanno*. Numerous other memorials and statues have gone up in his memory. The recently published book, *The Grunt Padre*, written by Fr. Daniel Mode, has served to inspire those who hunger for stories of heroism.

Almost forty years later, Corporal Ray Harton can vividly recall that September day of 1967 as Operation Swift unfolded in the dense foliage of a Vietnam jungle. On the previous day, Navy Chaplain Vincent Capodanno moved tirelessly through the region celebrating Sunday Mass for three battalions of the Fifth Marine Regiment. Attending one of those Masses was like "overhearing two friends talk," remembers Lieutenant Jerry G. Pendas. "He never tried to make me a Catholic but there was clearly a special presence about him. He constantly sought out Marines to listen to them and talk with them."

Father Capodanno's ultimate sacrifice given in the heat of battle reveals the transforming power of Christian love in the most unlikely of places—the terrifying chaos of a bloodstained battlefield.

Vincent Capodanno's Medal of Honor citation reads as follows:

> *For conspicuous gallantry and intrepidity at the risk of*
> *his life above and beyond the call of duty as Chaplain*
> *of the 3rd Battalion, in connection with operations*
> *against enemy forces. In response to reports that the*
> *2nd platoon of M Company was in danger of being overrun*
> *by a massed enemy assaulting force, Lt. Capodanno left*
> *the relative safety of the company command post and ran*
> *through an open area raked with fire, directly to the*

beleaguered platoon. Disregarding the enemy small-arms,
automatic weapons and mortar fire, he moved about the
battlefield administering last rites to the dying and
giving medical aid to the wounded. When an exploding
mortar round inflicted painful multiple wounds to his
arms and legs and severed a portion of his right hand,
he steadfastly refused all medical aid. Instead, he
directed the corpsmen to help their wounded comrades
and, with calm vigor, continued to move, about the
battlefield as he provided encouragement by voice and
example to the valiant Marines. Upon encountering a
wounded corpsman in the direct line of fire of an
enemy machine gunner positioned approximately 15
yards away, Lt. Capodanno rushed in a daring attempt to
and assist the mortally wounded corpsman. At that
instant, only inches away from his goal, he was struck
down by a burst of machinegun fire. By his heroic
conduct on the battlefield, and his inspiring example,
Lt. Capodanno upheld the finest traditions of the U.S.
Naval Service. He gallantly gave his life in the
cause of freedom.

In the aftermath of war, Marines and soldiers returning home without fallen comrades carry enormous emotional and spiritual burdens. Corporal Ray Harton is convinced that Father Capodanno has helped him to carry those burdens even to this day. "To be a witness to Father Capodanno is the reason why we are still alive. I am convinced that I was allowed to live to witness to this holy man."

Fr. Capodanno is consistently remembered by those privileged to know him as a quiet man of gentle presence and few words. "He could have talked theology to us all day long. But it was his example and actions that spoke for themselves," observed Major Dick Alger. "His ability to relate to the Marines regardless of rank was inspiring. Whether you were a private or a colonel, you knew he was there to listen to you." As chaplain of the Third Battalion, Fifth Marines, First Marine Division, Father Capodanno's actions spoke loud and clear indeed. His life and his death follows in that narrow path of selfless sacrifice that marks the witness of countless Christian saints. And in recent times of violence, war and escalated conflicts throughout the world, Father Vincent's holiness continues to shine as a beacon of light and hope.

On May 21, 2006, at the Basilica of the National Shrine of the Immaculate Conception in Washington, DC, Father Vincent Robert Capodanno was declared a Servant of God, the first step toward becoming a saint in the Roman Catholic Church.

Vincent Robert Capodanno's name is located on the Vietnam Memorial Wall, panel 25E, line 095.

Americans love heroes. Something about them grips the American soul. Perhaps the attraction lies precisely in going against the zeitgeist of this hedonistic age. Heroes are outside the box. They do not fare well in a culture where real living has been reduced to prepackaged experiences and media-generated events.

They get lost in consumer mazes where they are constantly told to enjoy life. Heroes do not sign multimillion-dollar sports or advertising contracts. Heroes rise above mass markets and mass media and quench the thirst of postmodern man by speaking of honor, courage, and sacrifice. Above all, heroes, especially those in combat, rise above complacency, self-interest, and comfort. They completely mobilize all their resources, with the highest degree of dedication for a determined ideal. And that is why they are held in awe.

—John Horvat

ROY MITCHELL WHEAT

No Greater Love: Roy Wheat in Vietnam is a painstaking work of love produced by Charles L. Sullivan in 1992. Countless hours went into the making of *No Greater Love*. The production process is a story in itself. Mr. Sullivan is an archivist at Mississippi Gulf Coast Community College. I owe a great deal of gratitude to Mr. Sullivan for allowing me to transcribe the video into the following chapter.

Marine Lance Corporal Roy Mitchell Wheat was twenty years and eighteen days old when he threw himself on an exploding mine in Vietnam and died to save the lives of two fellow Marines.

What would cause a Marine to jump on a mine, killing himself, to save his comrades? Love. Love is what Marines use to overcome the feelings of fear, which are natural in combat. Marines don't fight for their country, they don't fight for the Marine Corps, they don't fight for apple pie, motherhood, Sally Lou, or Lost Overshoe, Iowa. Marines fight for their buddies. That's what Roy Wheat did. He fought and died for his buddies.

No military commander ordered Mississippi's only Medal of Honor recipient in the Vietnam War to make such a sacrifice. In an act of supreme devotion, Roy obeyed a higher power, and he did it in the name of love. It happened on August 11, 1967, in Quang Nam Province, Vietnam, far from his hometown of Moselle in rural Jones County, Mississippi.

For all the years since his burial, the flag of the nation for which Roy died flies over his grave at Eastabuchie near Moselle. A granite monument stands in testimony to his selfless sacrifice.

On August 18, 1990, one of Roy's friends came to Moselle for the first time to meet the hero's parents. Ernest Barringer, at the time a civilian living in Maryland, had been Roy's platoon sergeant in Vietnam. Ernie arrived too late to meet Roy's mother, Estella, who had been in the hospital suffering a fatal illness. But Ernie did visit Roy's father, JC, and they went to the cemetery where Ernie reminisced: "My recollection of Roy goes back to when he initially joined the outfit. He was a very quiet young man. He always volunteered to do things that other Marines would not volunteer for. Things that were not too pleasant. Roy was a real good man on point, who happens to be the man leading the patrol. It was his job to look for the enemy, signs of the enemy, or booby traps. It didn't take Roy long to become very good as the point man. For many, it took a few months of walking point to learn the job and to know what to look for. In Roy's case, it wasn't that long. It seemed that he had this knowledge already built-in."

Roy Wheat is of the blood of Southern Scot-Irish and English frontier families with a record of military service as far back as the War between the States. In 1927, Homer Wheat moved his family from Alabama to southern Mississippi. Homer's son, JC, grew up near Moselle where he married Estella Mae Jenkins in 1945. Roy, the first of their four sons, was born July 24, 1947. Roy grew up on a small farm in the Piney Woods. To make ends meet, JC worked for Jones County as a heavy equipment operator and still put in long hours at a nearby garment factory. Life was good for a little boy whose family included not only loving parents and three brothers—Wayne, John, and Dale—but also grandparents, aunts, uncles, and cousins. Best of all, Grandpa Homer Wheat, whom Roy called Papa, lived within walking distance of the Wheat home. Roy and Papa were inseparable.

School pictures recorded the passing years as Roy grew up in a world imbued with the spirit of a much earlier era of American history. He absorbed the frontier values of hard work, frugality, religious faith, love of family, and an abiding love of the land. By the time he was ten years old, he was hunting alone in the Bay, a large forbidding swamp located between the Wheat place and Moselle. Many times he entered the snake-, alligator-, and mosquito-infested swamp where many squirrel, opossum, and raccoon fell victim to his deadly aim.

Roy began his training for Vietnam in the hot summer days and humid summer nights of his youth in the Bay. On May 16, 1963, Roy graduated from the Moselle Attendance Center, advancing himself to Moselle High School. At five foot nine and 145 lbs, he was too small to play football, so he became the coach's assistant on the Moselle football team. His ability for treating injuries and his desire to alleviate the pain of others earned him the nickname Doctor. While he loved football, Roy was an indifferent student. His major interest in reading extended to history and fiction related to soldiers of war. He dropped out of school in the eleventh grade, got a job in the Hattiesberg grocery store, and became friends with coworker Bobby Joe Strahan. "Roy was not the kind of guy you would think of as becoming a hero. He was more of an average person. If you had a hundred people out there, he would probably be the last guy you would pick as becoming a hero."

In mid-September of 1966, Roy, then age nineteen, went to Meridian, a city seventy-five miles northeast of Moselle, and enlisted in the United States Marine Corps. His parents knew nothing of his decision until afterward. Roy arrived at recruit training at Parris Island, South Carolina, in late September 1966. He described his experiences in a letter to his mother:

> I'm doing fine up here. You should see me in my uniform with my hair cut short. I go to church every Sunday morning. I have two bibles of which I keep one on me and one in my foot locker.
>
> I applied for communications but I'll probably just be an old jungle fighter like the rest of the men. Training is not too hard if you really want to be trained. Marines are trained for every kind of fighting there is. They train you on how to kill the enemy before they get to you. I don't know nothing about wounding a man at all. I feel real mean. That's a Marine for you. Tough and an expert fighter. I can tear a man's head off and he won't realize it for about 10 minutes. I qualified as a marksman on the rifle range and I was proud of it and so was my drill instructor.

Like all Marines, Roy rapidly developed the esprit de corps. In another letter to his family, Roy writes:

Today is November 10th, the Marine Corps birthday. We're 191 years old. Here's some background on the Marines and why they are known as the world's best fighters: The Mexican War and the Halls of Montezuma which is our Marine Hymn, The Battle of Belleau Woods where the Marines were named the Devil Dogs, Guadacanal, Tarawa, the Battle of Iwo Jima where the 3rd, 4th and 5th Marine Divisions accounted for more than 20,000 Japanese killed. I'm really proud to be a Marine.

Roy graduated from boot camp on November 29, 1966, and wrote his Mother:

Boy I sure look good in my uniform. I wish you could have seen me. I was lonely all day. I waited eight weeks to be free and I didn't even know how to act or what to do. I didn't even want any candy. I've got to say this, we had the best drill instructors on the island. When the busses lined up I really hated to leave and I believe our drill instructors hated to see us go. Mother, I just received my orders. I will go to Vietnam in March of 67. I will be home for Christmas and boy the girls had better watch out when I hit Moselle and Hattiesberg. Have the car gassed and oiled for me for I am going to ride. I can't wait to get into civilian clothes again.

But Roy remained in uniform throughout that last Christmas. He wore his field utilities during the day and his dress greens at night. He even ate his last Yuletide meal in uniform. On his final day of leave, his family drove him to New Orleans to catch a plane to Camp Pendleton, California. Roy's father, JC, recalls: "We had about an hour wait at the airport. We all had ourselves some coffee and Cokes and what-have-ya. At the time he was to board the airplane, Roy looked at me with tears in both of his eyes, and he said, 'Dad, I'll be seeing you.' And that was it."

Dear Mother and Dad, Camp Pendleton is a beautiful place. There are mountains all around us. I have been treated the best by the people here. Everybody can tell I'm from the south by the way I talk. I'm leaving for overseas soon and I'll be back in no time. When I come back, you can meet me here in California. Send me a picture of Dixie. You know a Bulldog is a symbol of the Marine Corps. Your old nutty ugly, hateful, idiot, sweet tender loving, kind son, Roy.

On March 9, 1967, Roy flew to Vietnam. He landed at Chu Lai where he joined Kilo Company, Third Battalion, Seventh Regiment, First Marine Division.

Dear Family, Well today is the 28th of March. There's one thing I dislike over here. You can't see the Cong until you're on top of them and you can't see what you're shooting at. You know they are out there so you just shoot at anything in the thick bushes and trees. You're bound to hit something. Yesterday we swept through a village killing 23 Viet Cong and capturing 25 suspects. We lost one sergeant. I waded about 200 yards in a rice paddy while a chopper flew above giving me and my buddies cover. The chopper was shooting Cong that were lying in the paddy around me. On the 27th of March, me and others were rear security for our company and tanks. The Viet Cong caught us out in the open and I could hear rounds hitting all around me. I opened up with a few rounds and then the tanks moved in and pushed the enemy back about 3 miles to the sea. Boy I sure did some crazy things when we got hit but you have no feelings for the Cong when you load your friend aboard a chopper after being all shot up or torn to pieces by a booby trap.

With his first taste of combat behind him, Roy's thoughts turned toward home.

Dear sweet Mother, today is the 5th of April. In three more months I'll be twenty years old. I bet I'm the only Wheat boy to reach the age of 20 and not be married. I never met anyone I ever thought of marrying. I guess the grass around the house is beginning to turn green. How the cows doing? I bet they are really growing now that they are getting plenty of green grass. Has Moselle changed any or does it still look the same? Hey Mama, have you heard the song called The Green Green Grass of Home? I want you to buy the record for me and keep it. I heard it over here and fell in love with it. How's the tractor running? I guess I want to be an old farmer and just raising and fattening cows and selling them. Some of these people over here are farmers just like the farmers in the states. They use oxen to pull a plow. We use a tractor. Sometimes it's not very pleasant over here but I'm fighting to keep America free and the people over here free. These people are human just like you and I are. I heard the Marines were being called baby killers for killing 14 to 17 year old boys. Well the hardcore VC over here range from 12 years to 75 years of age. The kids over here have real guns and real ammo and they are taught to use them very good. We've captured kids that looked like they were 10 years old and they turned out to be Viet Cong. Some of the women shoot as good as experts with the rifle. People in the states are crazy. They are sending blood and first aid to Hanoi and to the VC when we had two Marines that died because they couldn't get blood transfusions.

On April 10, Roy's company went by convoy to Chu Lai. As the convoy arrived, the Viet Cong shelled the base, and Roy suffered his first wound.

> *Dear Mother and family, I don't want you to worry any when I tell you this because I'm alright. We got to Chu Lai on the 10th of April and I just jumped off the truck when all of a sudden there was a big explosion. My feet left the ground and my rifle went up in the air and a piece of shrapnel tore a hole in my helmet and I got a scratch on the head. After that, I spent two days at a Chu Lai hospital and then I was sent out on a Red Cross hospital ship somewhere out in the South China Sea. The doctors are really nice and the nurses on board come around and talk and mail your letters. I'll be back with my company pretty soon.*

Roy Wheat joined his company on a hill near Da Nang just before Mother's Day.

> *Happy Mother's Day to you. I bet you thought I forgot but I fooled you. All I have that I can send you is a c-ration can opener that I have and it's not the best gift in the world but it's better than nothing. The can opener's technical name is a p-38. We call it a John Wayne. I don't know why it's called that. See if you can open a can of beans with it. We're sitting on Hill 55, about four miles west of Da Nang. There's 36 Marines on this hill and two M-60 machine guns and two Ontos. So we have a lot of fire power. We have a lot of barbed wire that is impossible to get through. I'm sitting here watching jets drop their bombs. It's really a sight to watch just like in the movies. Also, Marine fighter pilots really got guts. They come down about a hundred feet off the ground and drop their bombs and then they take off for another run. Those new phantom jets can fly as low as a chopper and as fast as speeds of up to two thousand miles per hour. There are fighter planes and bombers in the air 24 hours a day. We called in for an air strike on an enemy bunker from which we were being fired at and within 2 minutes we saw jets streaking through the sky above us. The enemy bunker took a direct hit with a 250 lb bomb.*

After a move from Hill 55 to Hill 10, Roy wrote a letter to his old friend, Bobby Joe Strahan.

> *Well Bobby Joe, we've moved up on Hill 10 about five or six miles southwest of Da Nang. There's a river by our hill and we are standing 24 hour watch on the bridge checking boats when they come up or down.*

We've got it pretty easy here and I think I'm going to like it here. We're getting three hot meals a day. I just got through cleaning my M–16 rifle and it's ready for action.

Do you like the picture of my new M–16? It packs a lot of power. We run a lot of patrols out in the field looking for VC so we can have a little fight with them. Yesterday when we got into a firefight I shot one out of a tree and I hit him three times before he hit the ground. I'm real good with my rifle. I've brought down VC as far as 500 yards. Your old buddy, Roy.

He wrote to his father about one of his most dangerous duties, mine sweeping.

Dear Dad, I started at 5:30 this morning for security for the mine sweepers. We walked about five miles from 5:30 'til 10:00 am. Traffic on the road doesn't open up until after the road has been swept for mines.

Other people from the Moselle area frequently wrote to Roy. He replied to Mrs. F. C. Brent, his elementary school teacher.

It was the third grade when you had me and my cousin Gene. I can remember those third grade years like they were yesterday. The Marine Corps is the best branch of service. I've got some good buddies and I have lost some good buddies too. On May 31st, we lost two Marines from our company. One of them stepped on a mine. I guess it was just their time and the Lord called for them. Your third grader, Roy.

On June 21, Roy notified his mother of his promotion to lance corporal and expressed an overwhelming homesickness:

I'm getting tired of this place over here. It's the same thing every day, seven days a week. It's like being in a dream. Everything don't seem true. All we do is sweat and kill all the time. Once in awhile I lose my balance. I guess that mortar round messed me up more than I thought. I'll be all right over here but they'll never be at peace over here. Not now or ten years from now. This place is strictly for the nut birds. I sure wish I could get some good ole southern home-cooked meals. You better have me some corn bread, peas, butter beans and okra for me when I get home. And a big slice of cake. I'm going to eat all the time I'm home.

At last the day that Roy had anticipated for months arrived:

Dear Mother, its July 24ᵗʰ, 1967. Today I am 20 years old. I got your birthday box. No mom, I haven't been in any firefights, oh for at least since the 4ᵗʰ of July, That's when we got sniped at from a village. Just think, 20 years old. It seems like only yesterday that dad was spanking my tail for crying too much and Papa was rocking me in his old chair. Boy how time flies. This is my birthday card I got from the first platoon. Don't let it get lost. I want to keep it.

Ernest Barringer recalled: "Roy picked up a nickname while he was over there. There were actually two nicknames. One was the Ghost, but the one most prevalent was Dead Man. The reason for it was because of his light complexion and his slow mannerisms."

Only three days later, Roy performed a death-defying act that earned him the Navy Commendation Medal.

Dear family, on the 27ᵗʰ of July at 8:15 at night we were moving to our ambush spot and we started up this hill and I was the point man. I found a wire that was running through the bushes and it was a booby trap. I grabbed the grenade and told the men behind me to run. It was a two second fuse. I turned loose of the grenade and ran back down the hill. It was the first time a booby trap was set off at night without killing anybody. Well mom, you can write and tell everyone about the great heroic bravery I did, ha ha. I'll sure be glad when I can get out of here and get home where I belong.

The citation for Roy Wheat's Navy Commendation Medal with combat V reads:

For heroic achievement while serving as a rifleman with the First Platoon, Company K, Third Battalion, Seventh Marines during operations against insurgent communist (Viet Cong) forces in the Republic of Vietnam on the night of 26 July 1967, Lance Corporal Wheat was acting as point man on a squad-size patrol. He parted some weeds in the trail, and in the process laid his hand on a pressure-release type wire of a booby trap. Before he realized what was in his hand he had already pulled the trip wire tight and all that was needed to detonate the booby trap was to release the tension on the wire. In a situation where many men would have panicked and run or yelled, Lance Corporal Wheat maintained his composure and calmly assessed the situation. Realizing what had happened, his first thought was for the safety of the men behind him. He held the trip wire taught and ordered the Marines behind him to clear out of the area. When he was sure that everyone was safely positioned, he let the wire go and ran back along the trail. He was able to get out of the casualty radius of the booby trap before it went off and no one was injured. Lance Corporal Wheat demonstrated exceptional presence of mind, calm quiet courage, and commendable judgment. His actions undoubtedly prevented injury and possible death to the members of the patrol. During the entire action Lance Corporal Wheat's conduct reflected great credit upon himself and was in keeping with the finest traditions of the Marine Corps and the United states Naval Service.

On July 30, Roy received his second and more severe wound.

Dear Mother, Dad and family, Just a few lines to let you know I'm doing fine. We were setting up an ambush Sunday when Charly threw a grenade. It got three of us. I got hit right in the tail. Isn't that a good place to get hit? Ha ha. Two of my buddies carried me about a hundred yards to get me medevaced out of the field. I'm at the 1ˢᵗ Medical Battalion in Da Nang. The doctor couldn't get all the shrapnel out so I guess I'll be carrying a little piece of metal around in my tail. Dad, I got the Purple Heart yesterday. It sure is pretty. The Colonel came around and gave it to me. Your Marine, Roy.

On August 8, 1967, Roy wrote his last letter:

Dear Mother and family, just a few lines to say hello and let you know I'm doing just fine. I'll probably be out with the 1ˢᵗ platoon later today. I sure will be glad to get out there and see some of my old buddies again. Be good and keep going to church. Tell those brothers of mine to be good. Love, your Marine, Roy.

For the next few days, Lance Corporal Wheat and two other Marines were assigned security duty for a Navy construction crew in Quang Nam Province. On the 11th of August, the three Marines were running a security check around the perimeter of the construction site. A well-concealed antipersonnel mine was accidentally triggered by one of the Marines. A hissing sound was an indication that a time fuse was burning. Lance Corporal Wheat yelled for his two comrades to take cover while he hurled himself on top of the mine and absorbed the impact. For his actions, Lance Corporal Roy Wheat was awarded the nation's highest award for valor, the Medal of Honor. The citation reads:

For conspicuous gallantry and intrepidity at the risk of his life above and beyond the call of duty, L/Cpl Wheat and two other Marines were assigned the mission of providing security for a Navy construction battalion crane and crew operating along Liberty Road in the vicinity of the Dien Ban District, Quang Nam Province. After the Marines had set up security positions in a tree line adjacent to the work site, L/Cpl Wheat reconnoitered the area to the rear of their location for the possible presence of guerillas. He then returned to within ten feet of the friendly position, and he unintentionally triggered a well concealed, bounding type, antipersonnel mine. Immediately, a hissing sound was heard which was identified by the three Marines as that of a burning time fuse. Shouting a warning to his comrades, L/Cpl Wheat, in a valiant act of heroism hurled himself upon the mine, absorbing the tremendous impact of the explosion with his body. The inspirational personal heroism and extraordinary valor of his unselfish action saved his fellow Marines from certain injury and possible death, reflecting great credit upon himself, and upheld the highest traditions of the Marine Corps and the U.S. Naval Service. He gallantly gave his life for his country.

Roy Mitchell Wheat's name is located on the Vietnam Memorial Wall, panel 24E, line 101.

Heroes in Heaven

Heaven's full of heroes
Who sacrificed their lives
In service to our country
So that liberty survives.
Uniforms of blue or gray,
Khaki or olive green;
Skin of every color;
Young and old and in between.

They fought in many places—
Spanning history and time.
Flags wave in their honor still;
In tribute, church bells chime.
In cornfields of America
Or on Europe's distant shore,
Pacific island paradise
Or Chosen Reservoir.

In blowing desert sands
Or in jungle's stifling heat,
In Navy ships or in the air,
Or Fallujah's dusty streets.
It doesn't matter where they fell
Or if we know each name.
What matters is to know that
When their nation called, they came.

Grateful for their service,
For the precious blood they spilled;
For their sacrifice and courage,
And the duty they fulfilled.
Yes, heaven's full of heroes—
Now part of history.
We treasure what they gave to us—
The gift of liberty.

Janet A. Norwood

Thomas Elbert Creek

I would like to thank the Virtual Wall website for a wonderful memorial to Thomas Creek. I would also like to thank *Leatherneck* magazine and *Vietnam* magazine for their outstanding article on Thomas Creek's heroic sacrifice.

There can never be "too much" done to honor those that have fallen in battle. This country has thousands of parks, buildings, highways, and even battleships named after some of our war heroes. My hat is off to those great citizens that spearhead such events. The Amarillo, Texas, Veterans Affairs Health Care System honored Medal of Honor recipient Thomas E. Creek by renaming the local Department of Veterans Affairs Medical Center after him on Veterans Day 2005.

Tom Creek was born on April 7, 1950, in Joplin, Missouri. He was the second of three sons of Ross and Bobbie Creek. With brothers Ross Jr. and Roy, Tom grew up in a struggling family that did not rise above poverty during Tom's lifetime. Bobbie Creek had her three sons by the time she was nineteen, and the strain of her youth added to the family's economic turmoil. Nonetheless, the struggles that accompanied Tom's short life seem to have only magnified the sound qualities in his character. These qualities would come to bear during the Vietnam War, when Tom became one of only fifty-seven Marines to receive the Medal of Honor.

Tom and his family left the Midwest for Amarillo, Texas, to be near Tom's grandparents and extended family. The friends Tom made in Amarillo have described him as cool and courageous, a Steve McQueen-type guy. In his youngest years, this courage was exhibited in a youthful brashness that occasionally landed him in trouble. In the military, however, it was transformed into bravery that he revealed in a selfless display of brotherhood for his fellow Marines.

For a time, Ross Creek Sr. traded driving a truck for roofing homes and businesses in the Amarillo area: Tom and Ross Jr. did the roofing, and their father did the scheduling. While roofing the barracks at the Amarillo airbase in the mid-1960s, Ross Jr. slipped and began sliding toward what would have been serious injury at the least, and could easily have been death. Just as he reached the edge of the roof, Tom reached out and grabbed his brother, pulling him to safety.

With his brother safe, Tom simply continued roofing the building as if nothing had happened. According to Ross Jr., "It was nothing to him—it was just like he was helping me. He didn't even appear to have thought about it. He just grabbed me in a split second."

At various times Tom drove an ice cream truck, pumped gas, and did restaurant work. His last job prior to enlisting into the Marine Corps was at Denny's restaurant on Route 66 in Amarillo. It was while he worked there that Tom bought his first and only car, a black-and-white four-door Ford Fairlane. Because of his hard work, Tom was able to pay the car off in just two payments. He was proud of his car, and in his spare time, Tom would take it to Thompson Park, a public park in Amarillo, and polish it from bumper to bumper. Meanwhile, as Tom grew up in Texas, the war in Vietnam began to rage.

When Tom dropped out of Palo Duro High School as a junior and joined the Marines, he was one of many who quit school in order to join the service. In January 1968, Tom reported to Marine Corps Recruit Depot, San Diego. During his boot camp training, Tom's hours were crowded with close order drill and military subjects that were of little concern to him a few short weeks before.

It seemed like the drill instructors were in his face, barking orders from sunup to sundown. When one recruit made a mistake, all paid the consequence. He did more push-ups in one day than throughout elementary and high school. By the time lights went out at 10:00 p.m., Tom was so exhausted that he couldn't sleep. Often, during those sleepless hours, Tom would pull a flashlight out of his footlocker and hide the light under his blanket and write home. In those letters, he would try to discourage his younger brother Roy from joining him in the service. Roy dreamed of following in Tom's footsteps. In a letter dated January 19, Tom wrote: *"Dad, tell Roy to be careful and stay out of the Marine Corps. It's bad. I don't like it like I thought I would."* Only a day later, Tom wrote: *"I wish now I'd stayed home. But I guess I like it as much as the other guys."*

Tom completed boot camp in March 1968. He then received individual combat training with Company A, First Battalion, Second Infantry Training Regiment at Camp Pendleton in April and basic infantry training with Rifle Training Company, Basic Infantry Training Battalion, Second Infantry Training Regiment in May. Tom was promoted to private first class in June.

Tom arrived in Vietnam on July 4, 1968. He was assigned to Company E, Second Battalion, Twenty-Seventh Marines, Regimental Landing Team 27, First Marine Division as a rifleman. Once he actually began taking part in the war, his pleas to keep Roy out of the Marines were only intensified. In the fall of 1968, Tom wrote: *"I can't hear out of my right ear at all because of this damn place . . . I have scars all over my face from bombs and gun powder, and I look like I'm 40 years old. I smoke three packs of cigarettes a day because my nerves are so shot I can't even hold a cup of coffee in my hand."* In another letter to Roy, also in the fall of 1968, Tom wrote: *"I'm not telling you a bunch of shit. This place is hell. Please, for God's sake, please wait until I get home and see me before you make the mistake of your life."*

Tom's warnings for Roy were interspersed with the many letters of encouragement he wrote to his mother and father. In another letter he wrote: *"Mother, don't cry anymore. I'll come back home, okay? Just don't worry about me. I sure love you and daddy and I don't want you to cry for me all the time. I think about you all the time."*

In the letters Tom sent to his mother, he also shared everything from the happy news of his scheduled baptism to his childlike hunger for ice cream. He told her that when he came home, he planned to eat *"ice cream every day and every night."*

In some ways Tom was simultaneously a boy and a man; he longed for ice cream and remained determined to kill the enemy while in Nam. Thus, he earned the nickname Billy the Kid from his fellow Marines—because he was so young yet had killed so many Viet Cong and NVA. In other ways, Tom was all man. The boy who had gotten into trouble from time to time as a youngster was now the Marine whose platoon leader said, "Lance Corporal Creek was proud of being a Marine. In doing his job, he often went the extra mile. I never had any problems with him. His record was unblemished."

Tom performed his duties so well in Vietnam that in September of 1968, he was assigned fire team leader, and in November, he was promoted to lance corporal. He was also considered for squad leader only six months into his tour. That prospect laid heavily on him: *"I may be squad leader before long,"* he wrote home. *"I sure hope not. That's a real bad job to take [responsibility] of all those guys' lives."* As much as Tom wanted to do well in Vietnam, he knew that the better he did, the more exposure there would be to danger for both himself and the men he fought beside.

The horrific cost that could befall a squad leader became deeply ingrained in Tom's mind during the last week of January 1969, when he wrote to his father that he had spent part of a day retrieving the bodies of some fellow Marines who had been killed in an ambush. Just as Tom had spent the previous six months worrying more about his brothers than himself and trying to convince them to stay away from Vietnam, in early 1969, he concerned himself more with the safety of his fellow Marines than his own advancement.

On Friday, February 13, 1969, a convoy was hastily formed to resupply the Vandergrift Combat Base near Cam Lo in South Vietnam. The convoy's mission was vital since the base was out of food, water, medical supplies, and almost out of ammunition. Sergeant Gene McPherson was in charge of the squad that was hastily put together to provide security for the convoy. As the squad was being pieced together, they stopped off to pick up a few extra Marines to round out their unit. These other Marines were substitutes. One of them was Thomas Creek. There was not a Marine in the convoy with whom Tom was familiar; he simply volunteered for the job because he knew that the supplies had to be delivered to the troops fighting farther north. As the convoy was driving the notoriously dangerous Route 9, on its way to the combat base with supplies and ammunition on board, the lead truck hit a land mine. "Clearly, it was an ambush," says McPherson.

Tom was in the lead when the convoy was ambushed near the Cam Lo Resettlement Village. Enemy bullets and mortars began raining down as Tom jumped out of his vehicle to take a position from which he could return fire. The other five Marines stayed behind to form a perimeter around the other trucks.

As Tom engaged the enemy with his M-16 rifle, he took a bullet to the neck. He began running back to the convoy. While he ran, with blood pouring from his wound, an enemy grenade landed near the trucks. What followed was simultaneously a typical reaction as well as the greatest action in Thomas Creek's life.

Just as he had locked eyes with his brother Ross when he was slipping off the roof of the barracks back in Amarillo, so now Tom locked eyes with Marine Sergeant Gene McPherson. And just as Tom had saved Ross from falling at the last minute, so too he now saved McPherson and the other four Marines from certain death with no time to spare.

Gene McPherson recalls, "We were too close together. You normally try to keep a lot of distance between you and the guy next to you in case the enemy starts throwing grenades in your direction." As he talks about how he and the other Marines tried to spread out, his voice chokes with emotion. It was then, says McPherson, that he noticed Lance Corporal Creek running toward him. "He was off to my right quite a ways, and he started running back to me. He was yelling, but I couldn't hear what he was saying. It was pretty loud with all the shooting going on from both sides. As he was running and yelling, he was pointing at this small knoll about twenty feet high. He continued running in our direction to get into our ditch for cover. I could see that he had been hit. He was bleeding from the neck."

Painfully, McPherson talks about how he saw a hand rise from above the pile of rocks where the North Vietnamese soldiers were hiding. In only a split second of time, that hand threw a grenade that landed just a few feet in front of McPherson and the other four Marines. McPherson says that Lance Corporal Creek had also seen the grenade being thrown. Choked with emotion, he says Creek looked him in the eye and shouted, "I've got it, Mac." At that point, says McPherson, it was as if the world began to move in slow motion. Creek, who had already been shot in the neck, threw himself on the grenade. McPherson says he saw a flash of light, heard a deafening noise, and watched Creek rise up into the air. To this day, McPherson says his ears still ring, and that ringing is a constant reminder of that terrible moment that changed his life forever. McPherson says that because everyone is connected in combat, everyone is like family. "If you hurt my buddy, you hurt me and you will pay." The tide of the battle turned. McPherson and the other four Marines, without regard for their own lives, stormed the knoll where the grenade came from. They found that the enemy soldier that threw the grenade. The enemy soldier turned out to be a woman. "We couldn't kill her enough times," says an emotional McPherson.

Lieutenant Blane Lillianquest, Tom Creek's platoon commander, was not part of the convoy, but he knew Creek. He said that Tom Creek's heroism was part of his character and not part of his training. "To make that decision in an instant, to give your life and roll on the grenade, knowing that it was going to kill him. That's something the Marine Corps instills into you. That's character that your family instills into you or your religion or your love of country or whatever it is. I mean that is truly the criteria for the Medal of Honor."

There is no doubt in Gene McPherson's mind that he is alive today because of Thomas Creek. And that, Lillianquest agrees, is Tom Creek's legacy. "It's honor and I would have to say it's those five Marines whose lives he saved. What have these five men been able to do with their lives? What joined happiness have they had with their wives, children, and grandchildren? And just the joy and happiness that life can bring, would not have been theirs had it not been for Lance Corporal Thomas Creek's sacrifice."

Lance Corporal Thomas Creek's Medal of Honor was presented to the Creek family on April 20, 1970, at the White House by Vice President Spiro T. Agnew.

The citation reads:

> *For conspicuous gallantry and intrepidity at the risk of his life above and beyond the call of duty while serving as a rifleman with Company I, Third Battalion, Ninth Marines, Third Marine Division in action against enemy forces in the Republic of Vietnam. On 13 February, 1969, Lance Corporal Creek's squad was providing security for a convoy moving to re-supply the Vandergrift Combat base when an enemy command detonated mine destroyed one of the vehicles and halted the convoy near the Cam Lo Resettlement Village. Almost immediately, the Marines came under a heavy volume of hostile mortar fire followed by intense small arms fire from a well concealed enemy force. As his squad deployed to engage the enemy, Lance Corporal Creek quickly moved to a fighting position and aggressively engaged in the firefight. Observing a position from which he could more effectively deliver fire against the hostile force, he completely disregarded his own safety as he fearlessly dashed across the fire-swept terrain and was seriously wounded by enemy fire. At the same time, an enemy grenade was thrown into the gully where he had fallen, landing between him and several companions. Fully realizing the inevitable results of his action, Lance Corporal Creek rolled on the grenade and absorbed the full force of the explosion with his own body, thereby saving the lives of five of his fellow Marines. As a result of his heroic action, his men were inspired to such aggressive action that the enemy was defeated and the convoy was able to continue its vital mission. Lance Corporal Creek's indomitable courage, inspiring valor and selfless devotion to duty upheld the highest traditions of the Marine Corps and the United States Naval Service. He gallantly gave his life for his country.*

Thomas Elbert Creek's name is located on the Vietnam Memorial Wall, panel 32W, line 025.

Taps

Twenty-four notes all loud and clear
Breaking the calm of those gathered here.
A flag-draped casket is laid to rest,
An American hero, one of our best.
The sound of taps
Brings a tear to the eye,
And we ask ourselves, "Why did he die?"
He gave his life so we'll remain free,
To protect and preserve our liberty.
Then seven Marines fire a volley of three,
"There is no better way to remember me."
Those mournful twenty-four notes
Have been heard once more
By all Marines in our beloved Corps.
So until we all meet at heaven's gate,
Those twenty-four notes will have to wait.
Then the day will come—
We'll look each other in the eye
And say, "Welcome aboard, Marine,
Well done and semper fi!"

Boyce Clark

GERALD HILBERT SAMPSON

After reading the memorials for Captain Gerald Sampson on the Virtual Wall website, I couldn't help thinking about what a great experience it must have been serving under his command. The Marine Corps thrives on its history, and it was men like Lewis "Chesty" Puller, John Basilone, Daniel Daly, and Gerald Sampson that set the foundation for the Marine Corps leadership of today and of the future.

Not only do I give thanks to the Virtual Wall, but I would also like to thank *Native Visions Magazine* and staff writer Allison Williams of Pembroke, North Carolina, for allowing me to use excerpts from their Gerald Sampson story published in 2005.

In the early-morning hours of August 28, 1969, Captain Gerald H. Sampson was deep inside the Vietnamese jungle a few miles south of the DMZ. It was his third tour of duty. As Bravo Company commander, he had instructed his men to set up camp for the night on an isolated hill. At the age of thirty-two, his men considered him a veteran, a lifer, who had enlisted in the Marine Corps at the young age of seventeen.

It had been a rough few months in Bravo Company, First Battalion, Third Marine Regiment, First Marine Division. On May 25, 1969, an ammunition pallet exploded, killing at least fourteen men. By August, Captain Sampson had seen just about everything during his third tour.

On August 28, Marines from a listening post (LP) came running back to the command post to report that NVA were approaching their position. Based on past experiences, Captain Sampson was aware that many of these young Marines on their first night operations were easily spooked. He sent them back out to verify the presence of the NVA. About five minutes later, gunfire broke out and the attack was on. Captain Sampson ran toward the fighting. He continued to move from one position to another, instructing his Marines to maneuver against the advancing enemy force, and in doing so, Capt. Sam was killed. He was struck by enemy gunfire in the middle of the night in a battle that would last until dawn.

For his actions and ultimate sacrifice during that fierce battle in the Quang Tri Province, Captain Gerald H. Sampson was awarded the Navy Cross posthumously, the second highest award for valor. He had always been referred to as Capt. Sam, and his men and fellow officers remember him as the best commander they had ever served with.

Corporal John Kamiski of Mayville, Wisconsin, was one of Captain Sampson's platoon radioman.

My first memory of Captain Sam was when he took over the company. We didn't know at the time that he already served two tours in Vietnam. We thought he was a hardass that wanted to make a name for himself by earning medals at our expense. It didn't take us long to learn otherwise. When he saw a squad bunched up down by the river filling canteens, he yelled at them to "Spread the hell out! One enemy mortar round could kill all of you." He was right. By staying spread out, one enemy mortar round or grenade would kill or injure only one or two. Captain Sam was very quiet and pretty much kept to himself. There was no fraternization at all with the troops. His conversations with other officers were strictly business. Tactical movement, positioning of his Marines, and engaging the enemy were his expertise. Many of his men are alive today because of Captain Sampson's leadership.

Steven Gugas was one of Captain Sampson's platoon commanders in Vietnam.

I joined Bravo Company in April 1969. I was flown up to Con Thien when the company was just coming in off an operation. I met our company commander, Captain Sampson, for the first time that evening. There was no welcome speech or anything. He assigned myself and another lieutenant by the name of Waters to platoons. I was given 2nd platoon and Waters took the 3rd platoon. He told us that we would be going out the next morning on a sweeping patrol around the Con Thien firebase. We were to follow and observe. The platoon sergeants were in charge.

I think he had me pretty scared right from the start. My impression was that he was an old Mustang [commissioned from the enlisted ranks] and that he didn't like new lieutenants.

The next morning we geared up and moved out. I remember that it was very hot and humid that day and I was carrying about 75 pounds on my back. We had gone about six clicks [1 click equals 1 thousand meters] when I heard a loud explosion off to my left. The 3rd platoon sergeant had tripped an anti-personnel mine and was killed instantly. Lt. Waters suffered serious wounds to his eyes.

My first real introduction to Capt. Sam is when he called to our radioman, "Put that new lieutenant on!" He ordered me to make my way over to the 3rd platoon and take charge of the unit. I thought to myself, That's pretty easy for him to say since he didn't have to cross a minefield to get there. *Well I made it, took command, and completed the patrol.*

That evening, Capt. Sam told me that he liked the way I deployed my platoon and that we looked really good crossing the open field. "Good spacing," he said. At that point, I think I fell in love with the captain.

Captain Sampson and I never became real friends. He just didn't get personal with his platoon commanders. It was just business and keeping your distance.

On another occasion during one of my first solo patrols, the captain called up and said that he was going to order some H & I fires (harassment and interdiction). He wanted to verify that I was at the right checkpoint. Heck, it all looked alike to me and I wasn't quite sure of my exact position. I told him that it might be better to fire a smoke round first just to be sure we weren't too close to the fire zone. About three minutes later, the smoke round landed about one hundred meters away. There was this awkward silence on the radio while he waited for my reply. After about a minute of silence, he just said, "I guess that was a little too close, huh?" Then he called a check fire on the mission. All the way back from Con Thien I was hoping for a lucky sniper shot to end my misery. When I returned from the patrol and reported to the Captain, all he said was, "Gotta make the checkpoints a little closer, lieutenant." Then he broke into his little grin.

After one particularly hard patrol about six months after I joined Bravo Company, Capt. Sam called me over after we had established the perimeter and asked me to sit with him. He poured me a cup of coffee, and we began to talk. I don't even know what the conversation was about, but I do remember that it was the first and last time that he called me by my first name. That was my fondest memory of him.

I was the commanding officer of five rifle companies during my service in the Marine Corps. I know what a good leader is made of. Captain Sampson was one of the finest.

Every evening while out on extended operations or patrols, the captain would have us dig in for the night. As soon as it got dark, he would get the whole company up and move our position a couple hundred yards. It was a lot of work, but he just assumed that the NVA was always watching us and jotting down our defensive holes for a later night attack.

Another quirk was just after each meal. The Marines had to repack their C ration cartons and put everything back in them. Then we would put all the boxes back in the cases and stack them neatly. I finally asked him why, and he told me that the NVA and VC liked to enter the camps after we leave and look for leftover food and salt packets. He figured that if they found everything neat and stacked, they would think this is one hell of a disciplined unit and think twice about engaging them in a fight.

Captain Sampson also had a unique way of tracking the enemy. On his map, he would notate every enemy contact by time and position. He would also do the same when other Marine units made contact with the enemy. Whenever we would go on a search and destroy mission, he would know where to look. We all thought that the reason he could find the enemy so well is because he was part Indian. Cherokee, I think. Actually, he just worked hard at thinking like the NVA and Viet Cong, and it seemed to work for him.

Captain Sampson was well liked and respected by the battalion commander, Colonel David Herron. I was detached and assigned to the Battalion Command Post on Dong Ha Mountain for security. I often heard Col. Herron talk about Capt. Sam. The night Sam was killed, Col. Herron kept calling me on the radio to confirm that it really was Captain Sampson that had been killed. I was just a little busy fending off a battalion-size attack and was getting upset because the colonel was

tying up the radio. But the colonel liked Sam that much and was quite
devastated over the captain's death.

I have to assume that it was Colonel Herron that put Captain
Sampson in for the Navy Cross because no one ever mentioned it to me or
asked me about the action. I just recently found out about the Navy Cross
on the Virtual Wall Website.

But now, only a few remember. His name is on the Vietnam Veterans Memorial in Washington, DC. But Gerald Sampson's name does not appear on any state veterans memorial. Not in North Carolina where he was born or in Pennsylvania, his home state of record. He was laid to rest at Fort Rosecrans National Cemetery near San Diego, California. Gerald Sampson never married nor had children.

A small group is working to make sure that Gerald Hilbert Sampson will not be forgotten. His chapter in this book is one. A sister, Sherri Stark of Pennsylvania, maintains a website devoted to his memory. Another sister, Mabel Sampson of North Carolina, hopes to one day see her brother's name etched on another memorial.

Steven Gugas said that he had learned a lot from Capt. Sam on how to be a good leader: "I don't think there was anybody that didn't totally respect him and feel safe with him. I lift a toast to him every August 28, and it's been forty years. Too long to allow a hero to be forgotten."

Captain Gerald H. Sampson's Navy Cross citation reads as follows:

For extraordinary heroism while serving as
Commanding Officer of Company B, First Battalion,
Third Marine Regiment, Third Marine Division in
connection with combat operations against the enemy
in the Republic of Vietnam. In the early morning
hours of 28 August, 1969, Company B, occupying a
night defensive position deep in hostile territory
northwest of Cam Lo, was assaulted by a large North
Vietnamese Army force employing automatic weapons and
rocket-propelled grenades. In the initial onslaught,
the second platoon commander was wounded and his sector
of the perimeter was in grave danger of being breached
by the enemy. With complete disregard for his own
safety, Captain Sampson moved across the fire-swept
terrain to the point of heaviest contact, rallied the
beleaguered Marines, and began to direct their fire
against the advancing North Vietnamese. During the

fierce firefight, he continually moved from one fighting position to another, instructing and encouraging his men and ensuring that the wounded received immediate treatment. While maneuvering across an exposed area on the foremost edge of the perimeter, Captain Sampson was mortally wounded by enemy fire. His unflagging determination and bold fighting spirit inspired his men to heroic efforts and were instrumental in turning a critical situation into an overwhelming victory. By his leadership, extraordinary courage, Captain Sampson upheld the highest traditions of the Marine Corps and of the United States Naval Service.

Gerald Hilbert Sampson's name is located on the Vietnam Memorial Wall, panel 18W, line 004.

"Freedom is not free but the United States
Marine Corps will pay most of your share."

Captain J. E. Dolan
US Marine Corps (Ret.)

KARL GORMAN TAYLOR SR.

A big thank you to *Leatherneck* magazine and Duane Crawford for "A Marine Hero's Legacy: His Family Remembers" published in the December 2008 issue. Mr. Crawford served in the Marine Corps with Gunnery Sergeant Karl Taylor in Vietnam and Quantico, Virginia. I am indebted to Mr. Crawford for allowing me to use his story in this book. I would also like to thank Shirley Ann Taylor and her family for allowing me to further honor her late husband, Karl Gorman Taylor, a true giant of the corps.

The low, rolling hills and wooded valleys of western Pennsylvania present a picturesque view for visitors any time of the year. Proud and patriotic, the folks of tiny Avella, Pennsylvania, are descendants of hardworking coal miners whose livelihood meant enduring years of sweat, dirt, darkness, and danger to keep America's industries running. There are no coal mines now. There are no expensive homes, no shopping centers, and no signs of wealth. Instead there is peace and tranquility.

Avella is also the home of a Marine hero's widow and children. More than forty years has passed since one of Avella's finest was mortally wounded on one of Vietnam's many battlefields. Webster's *New World Dictionary* defines *hero* as "a man of great strength and courage, favored by the Gods and in part descended from them." Staff Sergeant Karl Gorman Taylor Sr. embodied these words. As the only member of the Twenty-Sixth Marine Regiment to be awarded the Medal of Honor during the Vietnam War, Staff Sergeant Taylor's conspicuous gallantry and intrepidity has never been forgotten.

On a lovely spring day, two members of Staff Sergeant Taylor's Marine Corps family journeyed to Avella to meet the Taylor family and to remember their brother-in-arms. Retired Captain Ron Hoover had been commanding officer of India Company, Third Battalion, Twenty-Sixth Marine Regiment during the early days of December 1968. Richard Townsend, then a private first class, had been one of the company's radio operators.

Sitting among a group of modest houses on a ridge overlooking scenic valleys, the Taylor home, like others in Avella, had an American flag flying in the yard. Shirley Ann Taylor warmly greeted her guests and invited them into her small but homey kitchen.

The Taylor family consists of two sons and a daughter. Karl Taylor Jr., the oldest of the boys; his wife, Diane; and a son, Steven, were there. Powerfully built and square jawed like his dad, Karl proudly pointed out the framed Medal of Honor and pictures of the Taylor kids and grandkids that are displayed in the living room. Sheryl is the oldest and then Karl. Kevin, the youngest, followed in his dad's footsteps and became a Marine.

On one corner of the wall, a beautiful large portrait of Staff Sergeant Taylor in his dress blues and wearing the Medal of Honor is displayed prominently. The painting shows his rugged determination and indomitable spirit. "From a picture of Dad in his blues, a friend did the painting," Karl Jr. explained.

To the two members of her husband's Marine family, Shirley Taylor began to describe the Marine she had married and lost to war. Born July 14, 1939, in Laurel, Maryland, Staff Sergeant Taylor dropped out of high school after three years. "His family needed the money," Shirley admitted. "Later, he saw the value of education and received a high school equivalency diploma. Because service to country was considered a duty in the Taylor family, Karl Sr. and his brother enlisted in the Marine Corps on January 15, 1959. They were promptly sent to Parris Island, South Carolina, for boot camp. Following recruit training,

Taylor was sent to Camp Lejeune, North Carolina, where he was assigned to Alpha Company, First Battalion, Sixth Marines, Second Marine Division. He participated in Mediterranean and Caribbean cruises, performing various infantry duties and training.

During his stint with the Second Marine Division, he met and soon married Shirley Ann Piatt from Avella. Haltingly, Shirley said, "Karl loved the Corps, but he found time for his family. He was considerate, a disciplinarian, a very good father."

Because he realized that Marine drill instructors personify the best of the Corps, he asked for and was accepted to Drill Instructor School at Parris Island in 1961. He was a corporal. "Being a DI's wife was stressful duty," Shirley recalled. "Hours were terribly long for Karl, and he had duty every other day. Marine wives don't complain, and I didn't."

His core values were apparent on the drill field. Retired Sergeant Major Pete Seagriff remembers Cpl. Taylor as extremely fair but firm and revered by every recruit.

Cpl. Taylor and Sgt. Joseph J. McGinty were junior drill instructors of platoon 258 in the Second Recruit Training Battalion. Sgt. McGinty was awarded the Medal of Honor in 1966, while serving with Third Battalion, Fourth Marines. He later was commissioned a second lieutenant. Sgt. Ron Hoover was a DI in the First Battalion. He, too, was commissioned from the enlisted ranks. In their wildest dreams, Sgt. Hoover and Cpl. Taylor never could have imagined being linked together in Vietnam in 1968.

During August 1964, Staff Sergeant Taylor began a tour on Okinawa with Golf Company, Second Battalion, Third Marine Regiment, Third Marine Division. After the decision was made to send Marine ground forces to Vietnam, the battalion was one of the first to land in Da Nang in early 1965.

Upon his return to the States, Taylor was sent to Marine Corps Base, Quantico, Virginia. Assigned to Officer Candidates School, his exemplary leadership skills and combat experience helped in training future officers for Vietnam. Like all career Marines at the time, he knew another Vietnam tour was inevitable.

"Karl's orders for Vietnam arrived in early 1967," Shirley said. "We made a decision to buy this house. He often said of Avella, 'This is God's country. We'll retire here.'"

Young Karl recalled those days. "Dad called me the skipper of the ship. The day he left, he instructed, 'Okay, Skipper, you're the man of the house now.' Maybe he had a premonition."

Shirley's eyes glistened as she described that cold January morning when Karl left for war. "We hugged, kissed, and said good-bye . . . and he left. There was a snowstorm. His dad and brother drove him to the airport. Karl wouldn't let them go to the departure gate. He really believed that we were fighting in Vietnam for all the right reasons."

On January 21, 1968, the Marine base at Khe Sanh was plastered by enemy rockets and mortars. Staff Sergeant Taylor joined India Company, Third Battalion, Twenty-Sixth Marines on that day. Captain William Dabney was the company commander. The NVA had encircled the base; the Marines at Khe Sanh were in for weeks of tough fighting. While performing duties as platoon sergeant and platoon leader, Taylor participated in the defense of Hill 881 South.

After the siege at Khe Sanh had been broken, 3/26 moved to the Da Nang area and was involved in several combat operations. Staff Sergeant Taylor had experienced many intense battles and close calls, but the worst was yet to come. His drill instructor friend, now First Lieutenant Ron Hoover, was India Company's commander in October 1968. "I needed a good gunny," Hoover recalled. "Karl was all that and more."

Idolized by his Marines, Taylor was called Gunny T. Second Lieutenant Chris Tibbs, India Company's Second Platoon leader, said, "Gunny was always helping, guiding, and teaching. He was what every staff NCO [noncommissioned officer] should aspire to be."

"Gunny taught us infantry leaders the tricks of fighting the elusive NVA and Viet Cong. In both tactics and weapons, he was the perfect teacher," 2nd Lt. Tibbs added.

In late November 1968, 3/26 participated in Operation Meade River. Launched during the monsoon season and in the mud and weeds southwest of Da Nang, the multibattalion operation was considered the largest helicopter assault in Marine Corps history at that time. Intelligence sources had indicated that four battalions of the NVA's Thirty-Eighth Regiment would be trapped inside a Meade River cordon.

As the massive encirclement gradually tightened, the fighting became increasingly intense and casualties mounted on both sides. The enemy desperately tried to break out of the trap. Late in the day on December 8, India Company was ordered to attack what was a series of in-depth bunker positions. The company fought to within a few meters of the bunkers. From these hidden positions came a torrent of unexpected accurate and deadly automatic weapons fire.

2nd Lt. Brian Webber, Third Platoon leader, was mortally wounded; his Marines were pinned down and taking casualties. Many of India Company's Marines vividly recall Staff Sergeant Taylor's indomitable courage, inspiring leadership and selfless dedication. Cpl. Filipe Torres, the platoon sergeant for second platoon who later would receive a commission and retire as a colonel, said, "Gunny T. didn't hesitate. He said, 'My Marines are in trouble!' He grabbed his M-79 [grenade launcher] and extra rounds, and he crawled through the hail of fire to the beleaguered platoon."

With a companion, Taylor repeatedly maneuvered across an open area to rescue Marines who were too seriously wounded to move themselves. Learning that there were other wounded Marines lying in an exposed area, he led four other Marines forward across the fire-swept terrain in an attempt to rescue the wounded.

When his group was halted by the devastating fire, he directed his companions to return to the company command post, whereupon he took his M-79 and, in full view of the enemy, charged across a rice paddy toward the enemy position, firing his weapon as he ran. Although wounded several times, he succeeded in reaching the enemy bunker and silenced the fire from the sector, moments before he was mortally wounded.

Operation Meade River was terminated the next morning. On that day in Avella, the Taylor family was beginning to think about Christmas and anticipating the return of their loved one in only forty-two days.

Karl Jr., called Skipper, was five years old, but the memory of the soft knocking on the Taylor door forever will be embedded in his mind. He explained, "Sheryl was in school. The light tapping came from the back door. That was unusual because in these parts folks go to the front door. There were two solemn-faced Marines and a chaplain standing there. I knew something was terribly wrong. Mom called Grandpappy at the mill and told him the bad news."

Tears filled Shirley's eyes at the memory of those difficult days and nights. Her voice unsteady but clear, she said, "This whole community was and still is family. We don't lock our doors. We take care of our own. We band together."

Skipper described growing up without a father: "Grandpappy Piatt became the father figure. He didn't make it far in school, but he was smart. When us kids got into trouble, he'd whip our behinds real good. Grandma was the mediator."

A proud smile appeared on Shirley Taylor's face. She said, "All the kids grew up in this house, and they all graduated from high school. That would have delighted Karl. But there is something else I want told in this story. The Marine Corps, Karl's other family, took care of us too. When we needed something, his band of brothers cared for us. Everywhere we went in Washington, DC, his Marines did the escorting."

The Medal of Honor was awarded posthumously to Staff Sergeant Karl Taylor on February 17, 1971. His wife, children, and parents were invited to the White House for the ceremony.

Laughing, Skipper remarked, "Kevin was four years old, and he figured he'd be the life of the party. A Marine sergeant was given the job of babysitting us kids. Kevin decided to go swimming in the hotel's water fountain in his clothes. Then, he tested the sergeant's patience by climbing in and out of the barrels of some big cannons. One morning he turned up missing. After looking high and low for him, we found Kevin on the Marine driver's bed watching cartoons."

During the awards ceremony, Kevin decided to liven up the proud but solemn occasion. Grinning, Shirley Taylor described the story: "Skipper shook President Nixon's hand, but Kevin had his own idea. He popped to attention and saluted, causing people, including the president, to chuckle."

While presenting a nationwide address a few months later, Nixon mentioned both Staff Sergeant Taylor's gallantry and Kevin's sharp salute. The president also said in the address that he wanted the Vietnam War to end in a way that would be worthy of Staff Sergeant Taylor's sacrifice.

Kevin enlisted in the Marine Corps in late 1983 and graduated from boot camp at Parris Island in early 1984. He retired as a gunnery sergeant in 2004.

In July of 2006, a ceremony was being held at the headquarters of Officer Candidates School in Quantico, Virginia. A building was being named in honor of Staff Sergeant Karl G. Taylor Sr. The guest speaker was retired Marine Lieutenant General Martin R. Steele.

As a corporal, Lt. Gen. Steele had been inspired by Staff Sergeant Taylor and, later on, as an officer candidate. Taylor had provided him the guidance, advice, and the needed motivation to continue his career.

Lt. Gen. Steele said, "During the Vietnam War, the protestors were better known in our nation than our heroes. The only people who cared about Staff Sergeant Taylor were his family and fellow Marines. Today we have come here to correct that oversight."

As Lt. Gen. Steele spoke, Marine veterans in the large crowd silently recalled their service with Staff Sergeant Taylor. Captain Ron Hoover, the commanding officer of India Company during that fateful December 8, 1968, action that led to Staff Sergeant Taylor's ultimate sacrifice, closed his eyes, bowed his head, and remembered.

Hoover has never forgotten Staff Sergeant Taylor's final words before Taylor rushed through the deadly fire. Taylor yelled, *"My Marines are in trouble. I've got to go help them."* After that day, Hoover carried Taylor's M-79 until he himself was seriously wounded and evacuated on March 9, 1969.

Retired Gunnery Sergeant Kevin Taylor helped unveil the bronze plaque that was attached to the outside wall near the entrance to what is now Taylor Hall, the OCS bachelor enlisted quarters (BEQ). The ribbon-cutting was done by members of the Taylor family, the commander of OCS, Colonel Robert Chase, and Lt. Gen. Steele.

Inside the BEQ is a portrait of Staff Sergeant Taylor in his dress blue uniform with the Medal of Honor around his neck, a copy of the citation, and Staff Sergeant Taylor's framed Medal of Honor. The display honors the legacy of a Marine warrior and leader and serves as a constant reminder to all the NCOs who pass through Taylor Hall that service means sacrifice.

Karl Gorman Taylor Sr.'s name is located on the Vietnam Memorial Wall, panel 37w, line 070.

I Touched the Wall

For all the men who answered the call,
    Ten years after the war, they've built a wall.
Names of the dead, row after row
It took recognition so long to grow.

I walked along and felt the chill,
Honor and pride in their presence, so still.
    With a lump in my throat and tear-filled eyes,
I touched the Wall and to my surprise,
    It touched me back, as if to say in a solemn way—

"Wanted to be among the brothers
    Not the chosen to fall.
Wanted back in the world alive,
    Not a name etched on a wall.
    Wanted to hear 'thank you'
For a job well done,
    Or a voice warmly saying,
    'Welcome home, son.'"

The men who went are being honored now.
Word got through to the world somehow.
Now it seems the anger is in the past
    And everyone is talking of our plight at last.
    The Vietnam War and its controversy
    Have taken their place in history.
    Before you leave we wanted to say,
"Enjoy your freedom every day.
    Don't ever discount your liberty
    For we've all died to keep you free."

    Yes, I touched the Wall
    And to my surprise,
It touched me back,
    Filling both my heart and my eyes.

Alma Olsen Amodei

Gary Norman Young

While browsing in a bookstore at a military base in early 2009, a paperback caught my eye. *A Corpsman's Legacy* written by Stephanie Hanson is a book that I could not put down. I was reading it at the same time I was purchasing it. I don't even know what I paid for it. I put a $100 dollar bill on the counter, and when the cashier counted the change out onto the counter, I was still fixated on the book. I grabbed the change and wadded it up and put it in my pocket as I was still reading. I continued reading as I exited the store and made my way to the parking lot, with an occasional bump-in with other shoppers. Once I got to my car, I sat down behind the steering wheel and finished the book.

Stephanie Hanson was diagnosed with multiple sclerosis in her midtwenties. Her doctor told her that it would be imperative for her to locate her biological parents to obtain necessary medical information. In her search, she learned that her biological father was a Navy corpsman who died in Vietnam before she was born.

Four and a half years into her quest, Stephanie not only obtained the cold statistics she needed, but felt close to her father who served his country heroically. Through the help of veterans, a Marine Corps commandant, and a United States senator, she learns of her father's world of courage and bravery as a helicopter crewmember in 1969. Embraced by thousands of veterans, she discovers the greatest gift her father left her is the legacy of healing.

I had the pleasure of meeting Stephanie Hanson via e-mail, and she was gracious in allowing me to further honor her father, Gary Norman Young, in this book. I highly recommend *A Corpsman's Legacy* published by Leatherneck Publishing.

Gary Norman Young was born in Portland, Oregon, on November 3, 1948, to Weldon and Jewell Young. Gary had an older brother, Ron, and a younger brother, Steve. Weldon and Jewell divorced when Gary was four years old. Jewell later married Delbert Newton. Weldon was pretty much out of the picture and stepfather Delbert became the true father figure. Although Delbert and Jewell divorced many years later and Jewell died while Gary was in boot camp, Delbert maintained the status of Pops to the three boys.

Even though Gary experienced two divorces during his childhood, he was raised with much love from his stepfather and mother. Delbert loved the three boys as if they were of his own blood.

Gary loved going to school. That's where his friends were and that is where he excelled academically and in sports. Gary always knew that he wanted to help people, probably in the medical field, and in order to do that, he knew he had to maintain a high grade point average.

Gary loved all kinds of sports, particularly baseball and football. He played the games with the passion of a professional athlete.

Gary's brother, Steve, recalls how popular Gary was with the girls. "It wasn't only his charm that made him popular. He had the looks to go with it. His eyes were the most brilliant green. People always seem to remember his eyes. He had sandy-colored hair that turned really blond in the summer when he got a tan. His crooked smile was also an eye-catcher. He could curl his finger at the girls, and they would come running."

Gary Young graduated from Wilson High School in 1966. After bouncing around from job to job, he realized that the draft board would be calling on him soon. He wasn't about to let that happen. He knew that he wanted to be involved in some type of medical program. Perhaps nursing or even dental. If he must serve his country, he'd at least do it in the branch of service that could provide him with the medical training he desired.

Gary entered the United States Navy in 1967 and attended boot camp in San Diego, California. Out of boot camp, Gary was given the MOS (military occupational specialty) Hospital Corpsman. Upon completion of corpsman school at Camp Pendleton, California, Gary Young volunteered for Vietnam.

Gary was quite satisfied with how his military career was shaping up. He was proud to be a Navy Corpsman, and he knew that once he got to Vietnam, he could make a difference by saving lives.

Hospitalman Gary Norman Young arrived in Vietnam on September 10, 1968. He was assigned to MAG-11 (Marine Air Group), First Marine Air Squadron, Medical Section in Da Nang, where he worked in the dispensary. Most of Gary's work consisted of routine first aid such as suturing, applying bandages, and inoculations.

Occasionally, Gary accompanied a medical team to nearby villages to assist in providing medical care to the locals. The team was provided security by a Marine infantry squad. The experience of helping the villagers was quite rewarding for Gary Young.

Gary learned a lot while in corpsman school, but being in Vietnam is where he perfected his skills. Even though he felt pleased with what he was doing for the Marines and sailors of MAG-11 and the local villagers, Gary knew he could be more helpful to the Marines on the battlefield. Gary wanted to make a difference while in Vietnam, and he believed the best way to do that was by saving lives.

MAG-11 didn't operate medical evacuations, so Gary requested a transfer to either MAG-16 or MAG-39. Those units were located farther north near the DMZ, and they did fly medevacs. That is also where most of the Marines were getting hit the hardest by the enemy. Gary believed that he needed to be there to save lives, to make a difference.

Gary Young sometimes wrote home telling brother Steve and Pops what he hoped to accomplish while in Vietnam and what he hoped for the future. His letters were better expressed on audio tapes. The following is a recording from one of those tapes that he sent to Delbert Newton a few weeks after arriving in Vietnam:

> *Hiya, Pop,*
>
> *Well, I've been here about three weeks now and kinda seems like time is flying by, but then I look ahead and still have a full year here. It's not too encouraging. Sure do miss all of you at home. Sure appreciate all of the letters and the tapes. Sure helps out over here, believe me.*

It's not too bad over here. Every once in a while—well in fact, it's just about a nightly occurrence now—we get rockets and mortars in. Got bunkers all over the place lined up with sandbags, so whenever we get hit we just go running for the bunkers. So far, been pretty lucky, nothing's been real close. Quite a few guys have been injured and killed around here, but the ones that are injured, they usually come to sickbay here. Been getting a lot of experience in sewing people up, a lot of first aid. The doctors over here are just outstanding, you can't believe it.

I was pretty lucky to get this tape recorder to play as well as record one back to you. It's one of the doctor's here, he let me come in his little private room and listen to it and record back. At the time, I'm at a dispensary and mostly it's all first aid work. I'm doing a few minor surgeries. Very minor, I must put in, but it's all so fascinating. You never stop learning. I think that's one of the better things about this field of work. It's going to be, I hope, a short year over here. As I say, the time is going fairly quick. We're always busy. We're working seven days a week. I'm on a three-section duty at the present right now. Besides seven days a week, every third night I work thirty-six hours. Gets kinda tiring, but time goes by pretty quick.

On the flight over here from California, we left from Travis Air Force Base, which is right next to San Francisco. Took us about four hours, and we got over to Hawaii, stopped there, refueled, stayed there for about an hour in the Hawaii Airport. At least I can say I was in Hawaii at one time or another. Then from there, we flew on into Okinawa, which I believe took nine hours. It's quite a trip. Got into Okinawa on the 9th, I think, of September. We left early in the morning on the eleventh. We were mustering all hours of the day and night trying to catch a flight to go on into Da Nang. We were on working parties and not really too much fun. When we left Okinawa, we stopped in the Philippines, Clark Air Force Base. Stopped there for about an hour and a half. Refueled and resupplied, picked up more troops. While I was there, I called Pete McKillip—you know, Moe's brother. He's stationed there at the Naval Communications Center. His wife, Kathy, is over there with him now. He's going to be stationed there probably until about next March, I believe. And if I'm lucky, I'll try to take R & R [rest and relaxation] right around February, I think. I'm not sure, but if I can, I'm going to try to get over there and see them. Be kinda good to see a familiar face.

Last Saturday night I had duty, and when we have duty, we sleep here in the sickbay. At about five o'clock in the morning, we caught about six rockets, and they were kinda close. In fact, one hit so close to sickbay it actually shook me out of my rack. Must have been quite a sight, scrambling for the bunker with nothing but my Skivvies on.

Hey, Pop? Now this is important. Get a notepad and write this down. I want some salmon. Nah. God, I miss it so much. Betcha I ate half that tray when I was home during my thirty days' leave. Sure was good, and I sure would like some. Probably spoil though, on the way over. I take a malaria pill once a week. As a matter of fact, I'd better go in there and take mine pretty quick, today's the day. And there's quite a few plague cases over here. We got a report that there are six cases of plague over on the west side of Da Nang. Quite a few rats and rodents over here, and quite a few of the Vietnamese people are getting bit by them.

As much as I dislike this place, I can feel proud to say I'm over here helping people. These people are so very, very tired of war and poverty. They live in scum. It's worse, I think, than the ghettos back home. So filthy. We're trying to do our best, but because of the lack of personnel over here, it's awful hard to get around to all the people.

Whenever we have time, I try to get into the villages to help the people. Truly interesting. The people over here really appreciate it. It's really hard to tell the difference between a gook and a regular Vietnamese person over here. They both look alike. Sometimes you don't know if you are treating a gook who will turn around and shoot you the next day, or if you are really helping the people that need the help.

Monsoon season is starting to set in. Boy, you ought to see the rain. Just comes down in buckets, and it just doesn't stop for days and days. Nothing like the Oregon weather.

You're going to hear these clicks off and on throughout the tape because I have to keep turning it off, trying to think of something to say. Kinda doubt it if I make it a whole hour's worth but I will try.

Not really much to do over here for entertainment. Usually, when I get off work, I try to catch up on my letter writing, or every once in a while, I'll go down to the club and have a beer or two. Not really too exciting. Soon as I got over here, I volunteered to fly on the med evacuation helicopters, but unfortunately this Marine Air Group doesn't fly 'em. Possibly in two months, I'll be able to transfer to Mag-39 or Mag-16, which fly the med-evac choppers. Kinda looking forward to that. Think it would be kinda interesting.

Boy, you can believe I'm going to be one happy guy when I get back to the States. Although it's a long ways away, still looking forward to it.

It's gonna feel kinda good circling the Portland Airport. On the way back, it's just like the reverse routine, have to stop at Okinawa and get processed. Probably take two days. Probably fly on straight into

California. Probably be detained there for about twenty-four hours at the most, and then I'll head on home for thirty days' leave. Then I'll be stationed somewhere in the States.

It's going to be kinda tough over here during the holidays. It won't even seem like it. But there's still plenty more Christmases to come.

Every once in a while, the corpsmen here get a chance to fly to Thailand. It's kinda like a small Hong Kong. From what I've heard from the guys, it's real nice. Looking forward to going over there. At least it will be a break to get away from this place.

Quite a few of the guys here at the dispensary are getting pretty short. One guy is leaving tomorrow morning, and a couple of the guys are leaving next week, and we should be getting some new guys in pretty soon. At least I won't feel like low man on the totem pole anymore.

I should pick up another rank up to E-4 while I'm over here. Possible, but very improbable that I will pick up E-5. Soon as I go over two years, which is in May, I'll be getting another pay raise, another boost in the check. It will help out quite a bit. And when I get home, as I say, I'll have quite a bit of money. I just keep thinking about that little sports car. It will be good to get around in. I'll probably pay all cash for it, but if not, I'll just make my monthly payments on it. Anyway, I should be able to make it one way or the other.

Wish I had a nickel for every shot I've given over here. Boy, I'd be a rich man: I could retire as soon as I got back in the States. Done a lot of suturing, putting stitches in. The other day, I sewed up a colonel. He had a laceration on the chin from some shrapnel. He was pretty lucky it didn't take his whole head off. I told him I would send him my bill at the first of the month. Laugh.

Most of the guys over here are pretty nice. Got a real good staff of doctors. They're really decent. They'll back up a corpsman in almost any predicament he gets into, and a corpsman's judgment is as good as gold, as far as the doctor's concerned. Really makes you feel good. I'm stationed right next to the air base, and I think that's why we're getting most of our mortars and rockets in here. Trying to knock out some of the airplanes.

I've been issued a .45-caliber pistol, and I could have got an M-16 or M-14 rifle, if I wanted to, but I wouldn't be using it that much, so I just decided to decline. A .45 is about all I could use over here. Anybody gets that close to me that I have to use my .45, I'll probably be too scared anyway. Probably have to pick it up and throw it at them, instead of shooting at them.

Boy, there are so many fights here between the Marines. They all go down to the club, and they throw a few beers down, and they really think they're hot stuff. The other night I was over there, and this one guy in the corner was just getting really drunk. And all of a sudden he picked up a can full of beer and took it and heaved it clear across the room, and it bounced off the top of this other guy's head, you know. Never seen the guy probably before and had no bitches with him or anything; he was just trying to start some trouble. Bunch of animals. Laugh.

Marines over here treat the corpsmen just great 'cause the way they figure it, if anything happens to us, you know, who's going to take care of them? They really respect the rate of the corpsmen. It really makes us feel good. We do as much as we can for them too.

Got a letter from a buddy of mine from Camp Pendleton. Just bought a new Triumph, and he likes it real well. He's a Vietnam returnee. He was over here for eight months, and he got three Purple Hearts. Oh, by the way, three Purple Hearts will get you out of the country, but I don't really want them all that bad, so I'll just stick out the whole thirteen months.

Anyway, things are pretty much the same at Camp Pendleton. Kinda wish I was still there, but I volunteered for this place and I'm going to stick it out. I'm repeating myself, but it's not all that bad, but it's nothing compared to the stateside duty.

Well, Pop, I know I got a lot of tape left, but I'm running out of words, so I'll close it off now and try to add a little bit more later . . .

On February 4, 1969, Gary Young wrote to Delbert and informed him of his new unit and new mailing address:

Dear Pops,

Just a real short note to let you know I have a new address. I am now with MAG-16. it's a helicopter squadron. I will be flying on med-evac choppers. I will write later and fill you in on the details. Please write if ya get a chance. I won't be able to send any more tapes for awhile. This place is so desolate.

Gotta go for now and get squared away. Hope to be flying soon.
Love, Gar

Marine Aviation Group 16 (MAG-16) was located near Marble Mountain, approximately fifteen miles south of Da Nang.

Once again, Gary is the new kid on the block. The old salts that had been with MAG-16 did not hold back with the hazing of the FNG (Fucking New Guy). "What kind of idiot are you to ask for this duty?" "You like being around a bunch of jarheads all the time?" "Charlie's going to cap a round in your ass." Gary never wavered at the good-natured teasing. He smiled and was quick to respond, "It might be your ass that gets capped, and who's going to be there to extract the bullet?"

Another corpsman, Walter "Rip" Tyrrell, was assigned to show Gary the ropes. Rip had an easiness about himself. Gary was a bit nervous about his new assignment, but Rip had the experience and demeanor to put Gary at ease. After all, Rip had been in the country for thirteen months and several medevac missions under his belt.

Gary was quite overwhelmed when he was issued his gear. The bullet bouncer was basically a bulletproof vest. Unlike the thirteen-pound flak jackets the Marines on the ground wore, the bullet bouncer weighed forty-nine pounds. Its weight made it extremely burdensome. The flight helmet weighed three pounds by itself. Its two sliding plastic faceplates, one tinted for sun protection and the other clear, did little to keep dust and debris out of the eyes. The green flight suit was made of Nomex, a fire-resistant material that provided a little protection. Flight gloves, also made of Nomex and leather, were issued but were useless to the corpsmen since they couldn't check a pulse or clamp a pulsing artery while wearing them. Gary was also issued a .38 revolver and a shoulder holster for personal protection as well as protecting the wounded.

On the morning of February 7, and after very little sleep, Hospitalman Gary Young put on his green flight suit for the first time. After a few cups of coffee and a cigarette, he was on his way to the flight line where he met Hn. Rip Tyrrell.

Gary and Rip would fly with Marine Medium Helicopter Squadron HMM-364, nicknamed the Purple Foxes, a highly decorated squadron of the Vietnam War. Medevac choppers flew in pairs. The lead helicopter, a CH-46, carried the corpsmen. The second helicopter, also a CH-46, called the chase, was there in case the lead had problems. The radio call sign for the lead chopper was *Swift 1-1*, and the chase helicopter was identified as *Swift 1-2*.

Gary and Rip received a warm welcome from the pilot and crewmen of *Swift 1-1* when they boarded. To Rip, it was just a routine good morning. But to Gary, it was much more. Gary was deeply honored by the greetings he received from the crew. He was one of them. Even though he was the FNG, he wasn't treated like one.

Rip began showing Gary how to arrange medical supplies in his many pockets so that they would be easily accessible when needed. He connected Gary's helmet to the aircraft intercom system, which would allow him to hear the pilots and other crewmembers as the mission progressed.

The crew chief began the start-up procedures, and the big rotors started to turn. Gary looked out the window on the side and saw the ground getting farther away. He finally got his wish. He'll have his wings in no time.

Back at Marble Mountain, it was business as usual. While helicopters and fixed-wing aircraft were taking off on various missions, ground crews were hard at work. A few hours later, a call came into HMM-364's operation center. The duty officer listened intently. He then relayed the message to the head of the recovery team: "Sir, Swift Medevac is down. *Swift 1-1* is down in the zone. No activity noted."

First Lieutenant Richard Hardin, pilot of the chase helicopter, described what happened.

> *I was the wingman on the day of the crash. We had flown about two hours of medevac when we were called and diverted to an emergency pickup. Swift 1-1, the lead bird, was approaching the zone when she received heavy enemy fire. The pilot, Capt. Ernest Bartolina Jr., radioed me and told me their flight boost was going out. The flight boost is like power steering in a way but is absolutely essential for flight. Almost immediately after he called, his aircraft became uncontrollable and crashed. I got within 200 feet of the aircraft within seconds but received such intense enemy fire and hits to my aircraft that I was unable to land. I called for jets and Huey gunships for coverage, and I managed to get to the crash site with medical personnel on the third attempt. I later talked to the doctor, and he said that Capt. Bartolina, three crewmen, and two corpsmen died instantly. One man, the gunner, was thrown from the aircraft prior to the impact and survived.*

Gary Young wanted to save the lives of Marines. He knew that he could best serve his country by doing so. If he had to spend time in this God-forsaken war, he wanted to make a difference. Gary also wanted to earn his wings. It is the policy of the Navy and Marine Corps that one must have earned one Air Medal, flown five combat missions, or eleven regular missions.

After several months of endless letter writing, Gary's daughter, Stephanie Hanson, received a large envelope from the National Personnel Records Center. Inside was a full copy of Gary's military records. The most exciting discovery was a citation and certificate for the following:

The President of the United States takes
Pride in presenting the AIR MEDAL
Posthumously to

HOSPITALMAN GARY NORMAN YOUNG
UNITED STATES NAVY

For service as set forth in the following:

For heroic achievement in aerial flight while serving as a Corpsman with Marine Air Squadron Sixteen, Marine Air Group Sixteen, First Marine Aircraft Wing in connection with operations against the enemy in the Republic of South Vietnam. On 7 February 1969, Hospitalman Young launched aboard a CH–46 transport helicopter assigned a medical evacuation mission southwest of Da Nang in Quang Nam province. Arriving over the designated area, the aircraft immediately came under intense enemy fire and sustained several hits during the approach to the landing zone, he was mortally wounded when the CH–46 crashed as a result of the heavy volume of hostile ground fire. Hospitalman Young's courage, bold initiative and selfless devotion to duty earned the respect and admiration of all who served with him and were in keeping with the highest traditions of the Marine Corps and the United States Naval Service. He gallantly gave his life in the service of this country.

Stephanie Hanson also discovered that Gary's first mission was, in fact, seven missions. Gary Young did earn his Wings.

Gary Norman Young's name is located on the Vietnam Memorial Wall, panel 33W, row 083.

Our Corpsman Is Going Home Today

Our corpsman is going home today.
He came through our aid station,
We carried him slow, our heads bowed.
For ours is a lost sensation.

The burial bag he's wrapped in
It's dark. It's damp. It's cold.
He's not a hero. Just a Doc.
But his story must be told.

He came to this land months ago,
His determination strong
To treat wounded leathernecks
That fight the Viet Cong.

His only job was to treat the wounded.
His mission, save a life.
His tools weren't the tool of death,
The bomb, the gun, the knife.

A mission of mercy they called it,
This sailor in camouflaged greens.
No hospital ship or dispensary.
Just sharing hell with Marines.

Some complained of climbing mountains.
They're commonly seen in this land
Where life or death of a comrade
Is the fate often held in his hands.

But fate is not always there with them.

Author Unknown

Humbert Roque Versace

I have been fortunate in acquiring new friends at my local PTSD (post-traumatic stress disorder) support group. One of those friends is Chuck Hazen. Chuck served with the 199th Infantry Division in Vietnam. One day, while attending group, I noticed that Chuck was a few pages short of finishing a paperback. I asked what he was reading, and he showed me his book titled *Five Years to Freedom* by James N. Rowe. Chuck gave me the book after he finished it. *Five Years to Freedom* was another one of those books that I could not put down.

A fascinating story of bravery, spirit, and determination. A story of James Rowe's courage and the courage of his fellow POWs. His description of his actual escape is as amazing as anything one would ever see in a Hollywood motion picture.

One of Rowe's fellow prisoners was Capt. Humbert Roque "Rocky" Versace. Whenever I hear the word *patriot*, a picture of Rocky Versace comes to mind.

Humbert Roque "Rocky" Versace was born on July 2, 1937. He was the oldest of five children in a close, strict Catholic household in Alexandria, Virginia's Del Ray neighborhood and attended Gonzaga High School. Rocky took on the role of father figure when his father, Humbert Joseph Versace, was away with the Army. He had a firm sense of duty and moral responsibility. Rocky's mother, Marie Teresa Rios Versace (pen name Tere Rios), was an accomplished author who would write "The Fifteenth Pelican," a short story that became the basis for *The Flying Nun*.

Rocky followed in his father's footsteps and enrolled at West Point, where he graduated and was commissioned a second lieutenant in 1959. Assigned at the Old Guard at Fort Myers, he chafed at the ceremonial duties and volunteered for a tour in Vietnam.

While attending West Point, Rocky Versace studied French. At the time of his graduation, he was speaking French fluently. In 1961, Rocky attended the Defense Language Institute at the Presidio in Monterey, California, where he became fluent in Vietnamese.

In 1962, Vietnam had barely registered on the American consciousness. There were no US combat troops, only a few thousand military advisors sent to help the South Vietnamese government fight a communist insurgency.

Versace was assigned as an intelligence advisor for the South Vietnamese Army in the Mekong Delta. He immersed himself in Vietnamese culture and the delta village of Camau.

Don Price was a Marine officer that met Versace while in Vietnam. "Rocky was tall, dark-haired, and handsome. If you were going to ask for a West Point cadet from central casting, he was it. Capt. Versace created dispensaries, procured tin sheeting to replace thatched roofs, and arranged for tons of bulgur wheat to feed family pigs. He wrote to schools in the United States and got soccer balls for village playgrounds."

When his one-year tour ended, Versace volunteered for a second tour. After completing his second tour, he was planning on leaving the Army. He was going to become a priest. He had been accepted into the Maryknoll Order and wanted to work with children in Vietnam.

In October 1963, Captain Humbert Roque (Rocky) Versace was with the Military Assistance Advisor Group (MAAG) as an intelligence advisor assigned to support Civilian Irregular Defense Group (CIDG) operating in An Xuyen Province (IV Corps Tactical Zone) in the Mekong Delta region of

South Vietnam. On October 29, Captain Versace made a liaison visit to the Special Forces Team A-23 camp at Tan Phu to exchange intelligence reports on enemy activities in the area. Captain Versace accompanied the attacking CIDG force with Special Forces team members First Lieutenant Nick Rowe and Sergeant First Class Dan Pitzer. Captain Versace was seriously wounded with three automatic rifle rounds to his leg while helping to cover the withdrawal of CIDG forces in the face of a determined and very heavy Viet Cong attack. At that point, Captain Versace, Lieutenant Nick Rowe, and Sergeant Pitzer, as well as the CIDG forces, were almost out of ammunition. Versace had seven rounds left in his carbine and was about to charge the Viet Cong in one last valiant effort to stop their assault when he was wounded. Rowe and Pitzer were also wounded, and all three captured by the Viet Cong.

After being stripped of their boots, weapons, and personal possessions, Captain Versace, Lieutenant Rowe, and Sergeant Pitzer were bound and led barefoot into the jungle by their Viet Cong captors, somewhere in the vast darkness of the U Minh Forest. Versace had his eyeglasses removed, leaving him virtually blind since his vision was very poor without them.

Upon arrival on the VC jungle prison camp, Captain Versace assumed command as senior prisoner to represent his fellow Americans and immediately was labeled as a troublemaker by his captors for insisting the VC honor the Geneva Convention's protection for captured POWs. The Viet Cong didn't acknowledge any protection guaranteed to POWs as required by the Geneva Convention and considered the three Americans to be war criminals. Soon Captain Versace was separated from Rowe and Pitzer and put into a bamboo isolation cage six feet long, two feet wide, and three feet high. According to Rowe and Pitzer, "He was kept in irons, flat on his back. It was dark and extremely hot due to the thatched roof and bamboo walls. They only let him out to use the latrine and to eat. What they were trying to do was to break him. They even offered better food and they would let him out if he would cooperate, but Rocky would not cooperate. They wanted him to quit arguing with them and accept their propaganda. They told him that they knew he was an intelligence adviser."

As stated by the DOD Prisoner and Missing Personnel Office (DPMO), "Captain Versace demonstrated exceptional leadership by communicating positively to his fellow prisoners. He lifted morale when he passed messages by singing them into the popular songs of the day. When he used his Vietnamese language skills to protest improper treatment to the guards, Captain Versace was again put into leg irons and gagged. Unyielding, he steadfastly continued to berate the guards for their inhumane treatment. The communist guards simply elected harsher treatment by placing him in an isolated box, to put him out of earshot, and to keep him away from the other prisoners for the remainder of his stay in camp. However, Captain Versace continued to leave notes in the latrine for his fellow prisoners and continued to sing even louder."

Captain Versace wouldn't give his captors any information other than his name, rank, serial number, and date of birth as required by the Geneva Convention and the US Code of Conduct.

DPMO records reveal that "still suffering from debilitating injuries in the prison camp dispensary three weeks later, Captain Versace took advantage of the first opportunity to escape when he attempted to drag himself on his hands and knees out of the camp through dense swamp and forbidding vegetation to freedom. Crawling at a very slow pace, the guards quickly discovered him and recaptured him. Captain Versace was returned to leg irons, and his wounds were left untreated. He was placed on a starvation diet of rice and salt. During this time period, Viet Cong guards told other US POWs in camp that despite beatings, Captain Versace refused to give in. On one occasion, a guard attempted to coerce him to cooperate by twisting the wounded and infected leg to no avail."

In February 1964, the VC cadre forced the American prisoners to attend a political school, which was a combination of two thousand years of Vietnamese history of repelling foreign invaders from the Chinese all the way to the Americans and their Saigon puppet government, and intense political indoctrination from the VC perspective. The VC concept was to repeat the same themes over and over so that after months of hearing the same lessons, prisoners would become "reeducated" to accept the communist view of their inevitable victory over the Americans and the Saigon government, no matter how long it took to achieve or the cost in Viet Cong or North Vietnamese Army casualties. Rowe recalled that it took two guards to force Captain Versace to attend since he would not go on his own. "I remember Rocky saying, 'You can make me come to this class, but I am an officer in the United States Army. You can make me listen, you can force me to sit here, but I do not believe a word of what you are saying.'"

Captain Versace focused all the anger of the VC cadre on him so that Lieutenant Rowe and Sergeant Pitzer might have a better chance to survive. By constantly arguing loudly with his captors in English, Vietnamese, and French, he caused them considerable consternation during the political school that was supposed to get the Americans to write statements disloyal to the US government and their South Vietnamese allies. Instead, they got nothing but very loud arguments as Captain Versace was able to take on three indoctrinators in three languages.

Captain Versace and the other US Army prisoners were frequently moved from one POW camp to another. In the case of Versace, he was often moved individually without benefit of being near his fellow prisoners.

Brigadier General John W. Nicholson participated in numerous operations launched to free Captain Versace and his fellow prisoners. In fact, on three separate occasions, helicopters were dispatched for rescue attempts, and all three times they returned empty-handed, taking heavy casualties on one occasion. According to Nicholson and others, villagers reported that Versace was paraded through the hamlets with a rope around his neck, hands tied, barefooted, head swollen and yellow in color, with hair turned white. The villagers stated that Captain Versace not only resisted the Viet Cong attempts to get him to admit war crimes and aggression, but would also verbally and convincingly counter the VC assertions in a loud voice so that the villagers could hear him. The local rice farmers were surprised at Captain Versace's strength of character and his unwavering commitment to his God and the United States.

On September 26, 1965, Captain Humbert Roque "Rocky" Versace's struggle ended in his execution. In his too-short life, he traveled to a distant land to bring the hope of freedom to the people he never met. In his defiance, and later his death, he set an example of extraordinary dedication that changed the lives of his fellow soldiers who saw it firsthand.

Sergeant Dan Pitzer, who died in 1997, told an oral historian, "Rocky walked his own path. All of us did, but for that guy, duty, honor, and country was a way of life. He was the finest example of an officer I have known. To him, it was a matter of liberty or death. There was no other way for him. Once Rocky told our captors that as long as he was true to God and true to himself, what was waiting for him after this life was far better than anything that could happen now. So he told them that they might as well kill him right then and there if the price of his life was getting more from him than name, rank, serial number, and date of birth. Rocky stood toe-to-toe with them. He told them to go to hell in Vietnamese, French, and English."

Witnesses said the unbroken Versace sang "God Bless America" at the top of his lungs the night before he was executed. His remains were never recovered.

Lieutenant James "Nick" Rowe escaped in 1968 after five years of captivity. He later made an impassioned plea to President Richard Nixon that Versace be awarded the Medal of Honor. He spoke for an hour at a private meeting in the White House, describing the prisoners' treatment and Versace's resistance.

Retired Colonel Ray Nutter, an Army congressional liaison officer, accompanied Rowe to the meeting. He recalled that when the meeting ended, Nixon, visibly moved, stood and hugged Rowe. Rowe told the president that Versace deserved the Medal of Honor. Nixon turned and told the liaison officers to "make damned sure" it happened.

The submission sat for two years before being turned down in 1971. He received the Silver Star Medal posthumously instead.

It took over thirty-five years, but on July 8, 2002, in a ceremony in the White House East Room, Captain Humbert R. Versace was awarded the Medal of Honor by President George W. Bush for his heroism. It was the first time an Army prisoner of war has received the nation's highest honor for actions in captivity. Versace's three brothers—Steve, Dick, and Mike—were present during the ceremony.

"In his defiance and later his death, he set an example of extraordinary dedication that changed the lives of his fellow soldiers who saw it firsthand," Bush said. "His story echoes across the years, reminding us of liberty's high price and of the noble passion that caused one good man to pay that price in full."

Humbert Roque Versace's name is located on the Vietnam Memorial Wall, panel 1E, row 33.

Sharon Ann Lane

There are some very interesting statistics on the Vietnam War. For example, 88.4 percent of the men who actually served in Vietnam were Caucasian. Only 10.6 percent were black, and 1 percent belonged to other races. The youngest man to die in Vietnam was sixteen and the oldest was sixty-two.

A total of 7,484 women served in Vietnam; 6,250 of them were nurses. There are eight names of women on the Vietnam Memorial Wall:

Second Lieutenant Carol Ann Elizabeth Drazda and Second Lieutenant Elizabeth Ann Jones were assigned to the Third Field Hospital in Saigon. They died in a helicopter crash near Saigon on February 18, 1966. Both were twenty-two years old.

Captain Eleanor Grace Alexander, stationed at the Eighty-Fifth Evac in Qui Nhon, and First Lieutenant Hedwig Diane Orlowski of the Sixty-Seventh Evac, also in Qui Nhon, had been sent to a hospital in Pleiku to help out during a push on November 30, 1967. Their plane crashed on the return trip, killing all passengers. Alexander was twenty-seven, and Orlowski was twenty-three. Both were awarded the Bronze Star medal posthumously.

Second Lieutenant Pamela Dorothy Donovan from Allston, Massachusetts, was assigned to the Eighty-Fifth Evac in Qui Nhon. She became seriously ill and died on July 8, 1968. She was twenty-six years old.

Lieutenant Colonel Annie Ruth Graham of Efland, North Carolina, was the chief nurse at Ninety-First Evac Hospital in Tuy Hoa. She suffered a stroke on August 14, 1968, and was evacuated to Japan where she died four days later. A veteran of both World War II and Korea, she was fifty-two.

Captain Mary Therese Klinker, a flight nurse assigned to Clark Air Base in the Philippines, was on a C-5 Galaxy that crashed on April 4, 1975, outside Saigon while evacuating Vietnamese orphans. This was known as the Operation Babylift crash. Captain Klinker of Lafayette, Indiana, was twenty-seven years old. She was posthumously awarded the Airman's Medal for heroism and the Meritorious Service Medal.

First Lieutenant Sharon Ann Lane was the only American servicewoman killed as a direct result of enemy fire throughout the Vietnam War.

Hostile Fire: The Life and Death of First Lieutenant Sharon Lane is a book written by Philip Bigler. I had the privilege of meeting Mr. Bigler through Facebook, and he has allowed me to use some excerpts from his book in this chapter. Thank you, Philip Bigler.

John and Kay Lane were married in Russel, Kentucky, on July 5, 1941. Shortly after they were married, they decided to move to South Canton, Ohio, where they chose to settle and raise a family. John worked as a truck driver for a while and then became a bulldozer operator. The Lanes had three children. All of them were born during World War II: Judy in 1942, followed by Sharon in 1943, and Gary in 1944. The Lane family initially lived in a small rental apartment but soon purchased a building lot just a block away. Mr. Lane personally undertook the task of constructing a new home for his family, doing much of the labor himself.

Life for the Lane children during the 1950s was fairly typical of the Cold War era. The children frequently played in the adjacent vacant fields, walked to the local elementary school, and grew up watching the *Mickey Mouse Club*, *Ozzie and Harriet*, and *American Bandstand* on television. Sharon had many interests, which included sewing and photography. She enjoyed bowling on weekends with friends and playing pool on the family's own basement pool table. As a teenager, Sharon listed in her memory book the names of her favorite rock-and-roll performers, including Fabian, Dion, Elvis, Paul Anka, and Ricky Nelson. Each night she would tune in to the local radio station and went to sleep to their music, enjoying the luxury of sleeping-in whenever possible.

John Lane enjoyed an especially close relationship with his middle daughter, Sharon. The two would frequently go on day-long fishing expeditions to area lakes and ponds, enjoying the solitude and each other's company. They also spent many quiet hours on Sunday together in worship at South Canton's Methodist church.

Sharon completed her early education at North Industrial School and then enrolled at the nearby Canton South High School in September 1957.

Canton South High School was a majestic brick structure, which had first opened its doors to students some twenty years earlier in 1937. Its spotless grounds were surrounded by acres of well-manicured playing fields; the classrooms were filled with books, test tubes, and maps, strongly suggesting that this school took both its academics and sports seriously.

Sharon began her senior year at Canton South in the fall of 1960. It was a magical and exciting time to be a teenager in America. The nation was enjoying a relative prosperous economy and was still brimming with pride, self-confidence, and optimism. The biggest story of 1960 and the topic of many classroom discussions in Sharon's senior government class was the hotly contested presidential race between Vice President Richard Nixon and Senator John F. Kennedy.

Peaceful sit-in strikes were common throughout the country by African American students protesting the nation's racial policies and demanding immediate progress on civil rights. Soviet premier Nikita Khrushchev was making ominous pronouncements in Moscow following the celebrated show trial of American U-2 spy pilot Francis Gary Powers. Fidel Castro, the young revolutionary who had seized power in Cuba, seemed to be moving incessantly toward establishing a communist dictatorship just ninety miles off the coast of Florida. Of lesser note was the news of a growing insurgency in distant South Vietnam against the corrupt administration of President Ngo Dinh Diem. Viet Cong guerillas were becoming increasingly bold in their efforts to liberate the south and had just formed the National Liberation Front, prompting the Eisenhower administration to commit even more military advisors to the region.

For seventeen-year-old Sharon, these international developments were subordinate to the more immediate pressures of her final year of high school. She had a rigorous academic schedule that, along with her government class, included classes in world history, psychology, sociology, physics, and

English. Sharon had earned a reputation as a solid, conscientious student who maintained a steady B average.

On May 31, the South Canton High School Class of 1961 gathered for the final time in the school's gymnasium for graduation ceremonies. The students were resplendent in their cap and gowns, optimistic about their future but a bit nervous about leaving behind the comfortable sanctuary of high school. With the closing of the ceremonies, the Canton South students hugged one another good-bye before adjourning to meet with their families and friends for private celebrations. Sharon Lane, like most of her fellow graduates, now had to ponder what lay ahead—it was time to decide what to do with the rest of her life.

After considering many options, Sharon decided to enroll at the nurses' training program offered by Canton's Aultman Hospital, located only seven miles from her home.

After a brief summer vacation, Sharon joined fifty-eight other anxious girls entering the freshman class at Morrow House, the school's combined dorm and classroom facility. There was a lot of good-natured teasing of the new freshman students by the upper classmen. The younger girls were initiated into the nursing profession by being required to dress up in outlandish outfits and wear demerit sheets on their clothes. They were expected to bow when they passed the older girls and endure good-natured, harmless hazing.

Sharon's first year at Aultman consisted of a lot of studying and hard work. She soon developed serious doubts about her career choice and was ambivalent about continuing. After completing a semester of course work, Sharon decided to take a six-month leave of absence to reassess her situation.

Sharon returned to Morrow House at the beginning of the next school year. The second and third years of the Aultman program proved even more intensive than the first. Sharon was assigned to work on various floors of the hospital during three-month rotations, concentrating on a specific discipline. Her daily routine consisted of working on the ward she was assigned and attending classes.

Since Sharon had reentered the Aultman program, she completed her course requirements before the other girls in her class. She successfully passed her state nursing board exams before graduating in April 1965.

In that same spring of 1965, Sharon Lane was beginning her new nursing career at Aultman Hospital. As a board-certified nurse, her primary responsibility was in obstetrics where she was assigned to work with new mothers, although she would have an assignment in the nursery. For Sharon, the days at the hospital soon proved long, tedious, and routine, consisting primarily of tending to the seemingly endless needs and whims of new mothers rather than applying her medical skills. She did her assigned duties well though and was well liked by her patients and their families. Her coworkers remembered Sharon fondly as a talented and gifted nurse, competent and professional. But still, Sharon saw her life as unfulfilling.

After just two years at Aultman, Sharon quit her job to enroll at Canton Business College and began training as a secretary. This, too, quickly proved to be a disillusionment, and after nine months, Sharon concluded that she wasn't destined to spend the rest of her life behind a typewriter.

In early 1968, Sharon announced to her shocked parents that she planned on enlisting in the Army. Although she had never expressed even the remotest interest in a military career, the promise of working as an Army nurse had a great deal of appeal, offering potential travel to exotic places and assignment to posts in different parts of the United States. Military recruiters were, in fact, desperate due to large numbers of nursing vacancies because of severe shortages caused by the ongoing Vietnam War.

On April 18, 1968, Sharon went down to the Army recruiter's office in Canton and signed the appropriate enlistment papers. Although her routine physical showed that she had a slight heart murmur, probably caused by a bout with rheumatic fever as a child, she was deemed fit for active duty and was instructed to report to Fort Sam Houston in San Antonio, Texas, in early May.

Sharon arrived at Fort Sam Houston as ordered. She had driven the whole distance alone in her black Chevy Corvair.

Fort Sam Houston functioned as the Army's primary training facility for inducting military personnel. The basic training program was intended to help doctors and nurses make the transition to the Army, to learn basic soldiering and survival skills, and to learn the rudiments of treating war wounds. Initially, the basic mechanics of Army life seemed daunting. Sharon wrote, "We have to learn to salute and learn whom to salute and all that. This major told us if you don't know who to salute to, 'salute anything that moves until you know better.'"

Sharon was commissioned a second lieutenant on May 2 and spent the next few days filling out countless forms to feed the Army's legendary bureaucracy. Her service number, N-2-237-550, became her primary identity embedded forever in her memory.

Early in basic training, it seemed all the nurses did was receive vaccinations, polish their brass, stand for inspection, and march around post in their obviously new fatigues and combat boots. In a letter to her parents, Sharon wrote, "Our marching was terrible, but it is improving by now. I still can't do an about face right. I almost fall on my face every time."

The nurses then began serious training in wartime medical procedures including triage. The nurses were even taught how to conduct emergency surgical operations, such as tracheotomies, cut-downs, and debridements. In order to practice these delicate procedures, anesthetized goats were brought into labs for each nurse to practice on. Some had been shot to simulate typical wartime injuries.

"Today we did the tracheotomies on the goats," Sharon wrote, "and did gunshot wound debridements. These goats were alive but under anesthesia, and they had shot them in the hind legs with an M-14 rifle, like is used in Vietnam. Then we each had to take a wound and play like surgeons and cut out all the dead tissue, blood clots, tie off bleeders and such. I enjoyed it and think everyone did. We won't have to do it in Vietnam unless the doctors get swamped. It is a good thing because we don't know enough about deriding. I was cutting away on this muscle and cut a fairly large vessel by accident. Therefore, there was blood all over the place. Our poor goat had 6 tracheotomies done on him, and he was getting in rather bad shape by the time we finished. Apparently they are put to death and then cremated following the class. Thank heaven."

The combination of good friends and intense military training made the time pass quickly for Sharon. She was ambivalent about finishing her six-week basic training course because she knew it would mean leaving San Antonio and losing the camaraderie she enjoyed with new friends.

On Friday, June 14, the base held its formal graduation of this small class of thirty-six. Twelve of the nurses were destined for service in Vietnam. The other twenty-four were detailed to hospitals in other countries and various hospitals in the United States. Sharon was assigned, as requested, to Fitzsimons Hospital in Denver, Colorado.

On that same afternoon, Sharon was packed, and her Corvair was loaded with twice as much luggage than when she arrived in San Antonio six weeks before. It would take her two full days of driving before arriving in Denver.

Fitzsimons Army Hospital was a large medical facility located in Aurora, Colorado, just a few miles east of Denver. There was no real military post nor were any troops actually stationed there. Sharon arrived on Sunday afternoon, and with orders in hand, the duty officer assigned her her living quarters.

The next day, June 17, Sharon formally reported for duty and began routine processing. Finally, after several hours, she received her primary nursing assignment. To her surprise and dismay, she was detailed to begin work immediately in the hospital's tuberculosis ward, isolation units intentionally located well away from the main building because of the contagious nature of the disease.

Roughly one hundred male patients were confined in the two male wards. The majority were young, energetic, hormonal, and quite frustrated by their confinement. There were many arguments and fistfights. Many attempted to go AWOL. It was both a ridiculous and frustrating situation. Sharon felt "just like a matron in a boy's school, instead of a nurse. It's almost as far from nursing as one could get working supposedly as a nurse."

Despite these serious misgivings, Sharon was promoted on schedule to first lieutenant on August 30. Her new rank was still a small conciliation, but it did little to alleviate her overwhelming feelings of discontent.

Sharon repeatedly petitioned her immediate superiors for reassignment away from the tuberculosis wards, but requests were either rejected or simply ignored.

After four months in the tuberculosis wards, Sharon was granted a transfer to the hospital's intensive care unit. It was far more interesting and serious nursing, but it proved to be more intense and emotionally taxing.

Sharon found that her work schedule was relentless. The nurses were expected to work up to six days per week whenever the hospital was shorthanded, which seemed a frequent occurrence. Furthermore, the shifts were always rotating, so that each week, it was possible to be working an odd combination of days, afternoons, and nights without ever being able to establish a routine.

In the autumn of 1968, twenty of her fellow nurses at Fitzsimons received their orders for Vietnam. Sharon quickly decided that she, too, would be happier in Southeast Asia. She wrote, "I have decided to put in for Vietnam. There, at least, you are busy 12 hours a day, six or seven days a week, and you learn everything. No time for static from majors. They don't go." At last, it would be an opportunity to do something meaningful and significant.

Despite the frightening prospect of being sent into a war zone, US Army nurses, in general, felt they would be relatively safe while serving in Vietnam. Most of the American hospitals, with a few notable exceptions, were in reasonable secure areas; and in any event, they would not be the primary targets of a planned enemy attack.

In late December of 1968, Sharon received unofficial notification that her transfer to Vietnam had been approved. The formal orders would not be cleared until early January. Sharon was excited and was relieved to know that her time at Fitzsimons was now limited. She could hardly wait to leave. "Finally got my overseas orders! Am going to Vietnam in April."

In early March, Sharon went down to the hospital's personnel office to begin her initial processing for departure. It was estimated that she would leave Fitzsimons around the 6th of April. She was granted a two-week leave before her deployment. On the 24th of April, Sharon reported to Travis Air Force Base, California, for a flight to Long Binh, Vietnam.

Sharon received a 2030 hours departure onboard a TWA 707 charter, along with two other Army nurses and a woman from the Women's Army Corps. The remaining 161 seats were filled to capacity with regular infantry.

At 0800 hours, Saturday, April 26, 1969, First Lieutenant Sharon A. Lane, US Army Nurse Corps, and her compatriots had finally arrived at the Long Binh terminal in the Republic of South Vietnam.

As Sharon stepped out of the relative darkness of the airplane, she was temporarily blinded by the bright early-morning sunlight. Almost immediately, the brutal heat of Vietnam overwhelmed her. It was unlike anything she had ever experienced, even during the hottest of Midwestern summers back in Ohio. Indeed, the soaring temperature was exhausting and draining. It seemed to press down heavily on her, forcing sweat from virtually every pore and soaking her uniform in just a matter of seconds. Compounding matters was the awful smell, a combination of unique aromas, all of which were obnoxious.

After being temporarily billeted at Long Binh for two days, Sharon caught another flight south to Chu Lai, home to the 312th Evacuation Hospital and now Sharon's home. The 312th is an Army Reserve Unit from North Carolina that had been in Vietnam since September 1968. After a brief welcome and quick orientation, Sharon was sent to the hospital's supply office, where she was issued new jungle fatigues, helmet, boots, and a flak jacket.

Sharon was to begin formal processing the following day. Her first assignment would be a six-hour nursing shift in the hospital's surgical ward to help her adjust to the time difference and recover from the long days of travel.

In early May, military intelligence from the American Division Headquarters predicted that there will be a major increase in enemy activity throughout the region. In one of her letters home, Sharon wrote, "They are expecting a big offensive from the Viet Cong any time this month. If it doesn't come, they say it is proof that the VC are losing strength. So I have my flak vest, helmet, and boots ready every night just in case."

For Lt. Lane, the transition to combat nursing was brief. She was initially detailed to work on the hospital's surgical intensive care unit, mercifully one of the few air-conditioned portions of the compound. Unlike her previous duties at Fitzsimons where she had cared primarily for retired senior officers and elderly coronary patients, Sharon found herself responsible for dozens of young men seriously wounded and facing potential death in a distant foreign land. It was an enormous responsibility, but Sharon felt both needed and welcome at the 312th Evacuation Hospital. "Would you believe I like it here better than at Fitz?" Sharon wrote to her family. "Here everyone needs all the help and friends he can get, so it is much more warm and open." After a few weeks of working the intensive care unit, Sharon went to Ward 4, which cared for mostly Vietnamese children.

After the two-week offensive by American forces concluded in early May, there was a brief lull in the fighting throughout much of the region. The 312th continued to receive casualties but in quick spurts of activity. Nothing compared to the mass-casualty situations of early May. Still, on June 2, the hospital reached an impressive milestone by treating its 10,000th patient, a feat made even more impressive since the 312th had only been in the country for eight months.

There was no siren, no alert, no warning—just a bright flash followed instantaneously by a deafening explosion that transformed Ward 4 from an operating hospital into a pile of rubble. The lights went off momentarily throughout the compound until the emergency generators started up.

Cannon Sample, a hospital corpsman, was watching a spectacular sunrise when he was blown out the door. After recovering from the initial shock of the blast, he found his path blocked by rubble and debris. He was forced to run around the building to another entrance while hospital personnel from other wards had already begun to work their way toward the injured.

The ward's beds, once neatly lined up next to the walls, were mangled and shredded. Blood all over the floor hampered the medical personnel as they threw aside the wreckage, frantically looking for survivors. A twelve-year-old Vietnamese child was found dead; twenty-four of the other patients had sustained additional injuries. In the corner, Lieutenant Sharon Lane lay motionless on the floor.

In the emergency room, Lieutenant Sylvia Lutz had been taking advantage of the night's quietness by taking inventory when the first rocket hit the compound. In the ensuing commotion, several corpsmen burst into the emergency room carrying Sharon's pale and limp body on a stretcher. The on-duty doctor immediately began to try to resuscitate her, but there were no vital signs, no blood pressure, no pulse. Lutz tried to start an intravenous drip, but her efforts proved futile, and an attempt at heart massage also failed. For the next several minutes, the concentrated efforts of the entire staff centered around Sharon. It was obvious, however, despite all the hospital's medical technology, there was nothing that could be done to revive her. A small piece of shrapnel had lacerated her carotid artery, and she had died almost instantly.

Lt. Lutz moved Sharon's body to the back of the emergency room and secured a privacy screen around her. Throughout the morning, whenever time allowed, the doctors and nurses paid their respects to Sharon, standing before the screen, heads bowed in silent prayer. The 312th had lost one of their own, and even in time of war, nurses were not supposed to die.

Sharon Lane's name is located on the Vietnam Memorial Wall, panel 23W, line 112.

Sharon Lane, the All-American Girl

She came to Vietnam not to fight or warrior to be
But to serve a higher purpose across the sea

She knew the hurt, the pain, the dying
Sharon came to heal them and to stop the crying.

With purpose in her steps, she made the rounds
To give hope to the soldier and to turn his frown upside down.

Whether it be the boy back home or the Viet Cong
She did her job with care—she knew this is where she belonged.

She was cut down in the middle of the night
A piece of flying metal took her life.

She died alone
So far from home.

Her life was taken from us
Sharon's presence we still miss.

Let us never forget that freedom has a cost
Sharon became our hero—our hearts are empty by her loss.

Sharon was the All-American girl
She was perfection in an imperfect world.

Remembered by Doc Kerry Pardue, a field medic in Vietnam

ROBERT BENNETT SWENCK

Being a combat veteran, I have a place in my heart for each and every man and woman whose life was lost in battle. Not just in Vietnam, but in any war the United States has engaged. What attracted me to the story of Major Robert Swenck, United States Air Force, is not what he accomplished as an officer in the Air Force, nor was it his heroics while flying CH-53 helicopters in Vietnam. A memorial posted by his daughter, Stacy Scwenck, on the Virtual Wall website touched some hidden feelings that I haven't felt in over forty years. I am sure that any combat veteran that reads this will know what I mean.

I am grateful to Stacy Swenck for allowing me to include her wonderful memorial of her father in this book.

Memories of My Father, a Vietnam War hero, by Stacy Swenck

How strange I felt reading that obituary! I still lived in our little brick house in Fern Creek, Kentucky, I still went to Fern Creek High School, and I still slept in my own bed at night. My father had died in Vietnam, his chopper shot down by a sniper on Thanksgiving Day in 1971. I didn't understand then, as I do now, what I had survived.

The morning after Thanksgiving that year, as we were eating donuts and listening to music, an unmarked car pulled up in the driveway. Two men in dress blue uniforms stepped out. All military wives know what that means, and the men had only spoken a few words before my mother collapsed on the front porch. They carried her crying to the couch, and we were told our father's chopper had crashed in the river and he was missing in action. Mom sobbed; I felt shocked and numb. I took my two little sisters, ages six and nine, downstairs to the basement and kept them there. We stayed quiet and listened, forgotten in the confusion. For two days we made sandwiches and stood apart, watching. Dad's body was recovered two days later. Mom cried some more. People brought us food for a few days and then we were left alone. Mom stopped crying and walked around the house in a distant stare. A dark cloud was in our house for a long time.

For months I imagined my father showing up at my classroom door to take my hand and walk me home. Even now, I still wonder if his spirit will ever visit me in a dream, giving me guidance I still long for.

Soon after his death, I remember running into mom in a dark hall of the house and her sharp intake of breath as she said, "You look just like your Dad." She searched my face and saw every resemblance—my cheeks, eyes, nose, and frown stung her heart. I couldn't help being a reminder of sorrow for my mom. Did we remind everyone we knew of Death, our faces omens of the grief Death brings?

We had been mainly sheltered from television images of the war. Besides, those men wearing camouflage running around on the ground were not my dad. My dad was a pilot, he wore a plain flight suit when he went to work. He was doing something "Top Secret" and the return address on his letters was fake. As far as I knew, Dad was at work on a very long mission. I didn't understand what war was. Then he was killed. As I grew older, I came to hate the Vietnam War and blamed the government, even though I had no idea about the war's causes and avoided any mention of it. I became a rebellious teenager, transforming hate into toughness. I grew bitter in my ignorance. Hating the war helped when I had to tell someone my father died fighting there. I couldn't say he had been drafted unwillingly; he was a career soldier who served two tours in

Vietnam. Joining in the belief that it was a bad war made it easier to get along with others who hated it, which was most everyone I met. I did not know then that my father had been a hero.

I found out about that from the Trunk. On Thanksgiving Day, 1996, the 25th anniversary of his death, Mom appeared and deposited a heavy blue trunk in my living room. She firmly announced that these were my father's things and were now mine to keep. She was finished with them. I wasn't sure I wanted the trunk, and I put it away in the closet. Many months later I opened it and found my father's blue uniform, several medals and a large stack of letters.

I had seen the medals as a child, set out on the bookcase in the basement. He had earned them during his first tour in 1969. Now I saw what they were: a Silver Star (one of the top medals a soldier can earn), three Distinguished Flying Crosses, an Airman's Medal for Valor (he was most proud of this one), eight Air Medals and a Purple Heart. I had read over 100 letters he had written to Mom and to us. I found out that Dad was a highly skilled Air Force chopper pilot for the 20th Special Operations Squadron (the Green Hornets) who was flying "sensitive and classified missions" on the real, secret front lines of the war. The 20th S.O.S.'s mission was to rescue long-range reconnaissance patrols on the ground in Cambodia during a time when both the United States and North Vietnam were denying any involvement there. He repeatedly flew extremely hazardous missions head-on into gunfire with frequent disregard for his own life. One time he and his men ran to a crashed and burning helicopter and lifted it up enough to free a man who had been pinned underneath. Reading the letter he wrote to my mother that same evening took my breath away.

Since opening the trunk, I have researched the war and asked my mother many questions. She bravely told me how they met and what kind of husband and father he was. They grew up in Okolona, Kentucky and met when Mom was about 10 years old. She wanted to play baseball with the boys and Dad said, "Aw, let her play awhile. Then she'll go away." They were high school sweethearts at Southern High School; she was a cheerleader and he was on the basketball team. He courted her from Western Kentucky State, and she followed him there two years later.

My search for information has intensified since September 11, 2001. Seeing the faces of those who had lost loved ones made me know I could not wait any longer to tell my family's story. I wanted those children to know someone understood their loss. I recently made several internet contacts with men who flew with my father. They are telling me stories of his bravery and skill, and about his ever-present wit. Everyone respected him. The day he died, he had flown in the rain to rescue 14 Navy men from battle. After sharing a turkey sandwich with them at their home base, he was flying back low under the rain clouds when a sniper's bullet struck him, killing him instantly in midair.

My own memories have surfaced. I remember him being tall and having feet so big I could sit on one and get a ride around the house. He and Mom had lots of friends and gave big parties. He would kiss Mom in the kitchen and squeeze her knee during road trips in the car. He affectionately rubbed my head until my hair shook, and he challenged me to always do my best in school. He taught us proper manners in a restaurant. His shadowy presence looming in the doorway was enough to make my sister and I to stop our loud nighttime giggling and lay quiet as mice in our beds. He was always telling jokes and could make anything sound funny. He told us that he earned the Silver Star by flying a general to use a real latrine.

When Dad returned from his first tour in Vietnam, he arrived at Standiford Field Airport still wearing his flight suit. The airport personnel made him enter the terminal through the back door so he wouldn't upset the passengers or be called a baby killer. I remember Mom and us three girls waiting just inside the big plate glass windows, watching each person walk across the tarmac, looking for Dad. Suddenly Mom flew around toward us and spoke quickly in a tone that made me know her instructions were very important. "Sit here, girls. Wait and don't move. I have to go meet your father at another gate." Mom's look was stern and fierce, but she wasn't mad at us. We sat wide-eyed for a long time, and finally there was Dad walking down the hall, Mom clinging to his neck. We ran and grabbed at his waist, his knees, whatever we could reach according to our heights. He tried to hug us all at the same time with different hugs. Mom needed a certain wife-hug, Heidi, a baby hug up in his arms and Lori and I, some little girl hugs. Mine came with a little respect attached since I was the oldest. Lori got the rough house since she was a tomboy and his favorite. We were so happy to see him.

However, when Dad got home, he was different. When me and my sisters jumped on him to tickle him, he growled and pushed us away. He turned mean. He got mad at the dog over an accident and threw it up against the wall. He broke a guy's nose at a party for making derogatory comments about the Vietnam War. Mom tells how he woke up from nightmares in a cold sweat. All he could think about was going back over there and that is what he did a few months later. When we drove him to the airport, I cried uncontrollably in the car. I did not know that would be the last time I would ever see him.

I am proud to be Dad's daughter. Mom deserves a medal of her own. She is an original Super Mom who worked full-time and raised three young girls up into happy, successful adults. The strength of both parents lives on in us. My sisters still do not like to talk about my Dad but one day, our children will be glad to hear about him. Bob Swenck never saw his three daughters graduate college or get married; he can't kiss his grandchildren or hold his wife's hand as they grow old. Heroes have historically fought for a good cause. My father was a hero because he believed he was defending the freedom of his family and country. He could not know he was jousting against the windmills of communism. The Viet Cong was a real enemy, vicious in battle. He fought hard and bravely and gave his life for his fellow man. He deserves the same honor as any soldier. He did not die for nothing. He died for his belief in freedom, because he was a soldier doing his job. I write this to give him that honor.

On November 25, 1971, two CH-53 helicopters of the Thirty-Seventh ARRS, call signs JOLLY GREEN 70 and 73, departed Bien Hoa Airbase to pick up survivors of a crash near Can Tho. During the pickup, JOLLY GREEN 70 took hits from enemy fire. After dropping off the crash survivors at Can Tho, the crew of JOLLY GREEN 70 checked their aircraft and decided it was capable of the return flight to Bien Hoa Airbase. JOLLY GREEN 70 was crewed by Maj. Robert Swenck, pilot; Capt. John George, copilot; T.Sgt. James Thomas, pararescueman; Sgt. R. L. Sneed, pararesueman; Sgt. H. Theriot, flight engineer; and A1C Thomas Prose, pararescueman.

The two JOLLY GREENs departed Can Tho in tactical formation for the ninety-five-mile flight to Bien Hoa to the northeast. During the return flight, they encountered a 100 foot to 300 foot overcast with moderate to heavy rain showers. At 1550 hours, while flying below the cloud cover, JOLLY GREEN 73 lost contact with JOLLY GREEN 70. When radio contact could not be reestablished, search and rescue efforts had begun. JOLLY GREEN was located approximately thirteen nautical miles southeast of Tan Son Nhut Airbase, Saigon, in the Song Nha Be River, near the town of Nha Be, Gia Dinh Province, South Vietnam. The aircraft wreckage was close to the east bank of the river. While the west bank of the river was secure, the east side was considered enemy territory.

Two crewmen (Theriot and Sneed) survived the crash and reported that the aircraft had been hit by enemy ground fire. There was a report from a local fisherman that a third person was tentatively identified as T.Sgt. Thomas.

Salvage efforts began at once, with Vietnamese divers locating and searching the submerged wreckage. The aircraft was raised with cables, and the bodies of Maj. Swenck, Capt. George, and A1C Prose recovered. While the wreckage was being towed to a more secure location, the cabling broke, and the wreckage sank once more. On November 27, divers once again searched the wreckage for Thomas's body, and the wreck was raised a second time for a further search. Thomas was not found, nor was he found during ground searches of the river banks downstream. His body was never recovered.

Major Robert Bennett Swenck's name is located on the Vietnam Memorial Wall, panel 02W, line 072.

"Regard your soldiers as
Your children and they will
Follow you into the deepest
Valleys; look on them as your
Own beloved sons, and they will
Stand by you even unto death."

Sun Tzu

NICHOLAS OWEN WAGMAN

I came across Nicholas Wagman's name while browsing through memorials on the Virtual Wall website. Aside from his Purple Heart Medal, he was awarded no medals of valor. Nevertheless, Nicholas Wagman was a hero. The impact he made on the lives of all who knew him was everlasting. A memorial posted on the Virtual Wall site by Nicholas's sister, Samantha Frishberg, says it all.

Another thank you to the Virtual Wall and a special thanks to Samantha for allowing me to use her memorial and to further honor her brother, Nicholas Owen Wagman, in this chapter.

An eighteen-year-old high school student from Nevada was assigned to write a report on one of the fallen from the Vietnam Memorial Wall before her class trip to Washington, DC. Nicholas Owen Wagman's name was randomly picked. Through her research, she found a sister of Wagman's. Her name is Samantha Frishberg. She sent a letter to Samantha asking for information about her brother. The following is a response to that letter:

Hello Jennifer,

Nick was born on the 31ˢᵗ of August, 1947 and raised in Ludlow, Kentucky, just across the Ohio River and Cincinnati, Ohio. Nick was four years older than me. He was a wonderful brother, always laughing and joking with affection.

He was also serious. He had a job working after school, on Saturdays and during vacations ever since I could remember. Nick worked on a local produce truck which visited neighborhoods in our small hometown of 6,000. He carried orders of groceries and wooden cases of Coca-Cola bottles into the homes of customers. With all of his tips, Nick always had a pocket full of change. I have fond memories of Nick's generosity. He shared his tips with me, which he referred as his "good fortune." Nick was polite with very good manners and all of the neighborhood women appreciated his kind smile and gentle style.

We watched westerns and the Mickey Mouse Club *on TV together. We also played yellow and red vinyl records on our portable record player. Nick often played and sang to the military theme songs for all the branches of the military. He was always partial to the Marine Corps Hymn.*

Nick loved his dogs, especially his first, an old black Cocker Spaniel he called Sammi. Sammi had been hit by a car and was paralyzed in the hind quarters. The dog couldn't walk but he got around just fine by dragging his hind legs and scooting all over the yard. Often, Nick would feel sorry for Sammi and pick him up. He loved playing with Sammi more than anything. Nick was as kind to animals as he was toward people. When I would see him being kind, and he thought no one was looking, my heart would break with pride. And for that, Nick was my hero.

We walked to and from St. James Elementary School together and Nick would always make sure I was safe from possibly being bullied by some of the older neighborhood kids.

Nick and some of his 8ᵗʰ grade friends performed a soft shoe tap dance on a team and they won a trophy for one of the school's performances. I also tap danced in annual St. Patrick's Day talent shows. We practiced in the dingy basement of our house. Nick would protect me from the icky water bugs and spiders that I was so scared of.

Nick loved baseball. He played in little league and in high school. Many times, he and I would walk over the railroad trestle into Cincinnati and catch a Cincinnati Reds baseball game.

On Sunday afternoons we would walk to the local movie theater. It was there where Nick taught me about all the different kinds of candy that was sold in the lobby. His favorite was Boston Baked Beans. We trick-or-treated together and he always knew who was giving out the bigger candy bars. I looked up to him as an expert on many things.

Being an Irish Catholic, Nick was an altar boy, attending Mass back when Mass was given in Latin. He also studied Latin while in high school.

I believe Nick's biggest love was his cherry red 1957 Chevy. He already had the good looks and the charm. He had a few girlfriends in high school. I don't think the Chevy had anything to do with it but maybe he did. On his car radio, he liked listening to the Four Seasons, the Beach Boys, Diana Ross, the Supremes, and the Rolling Stones when they first came out. In fact, from Vietnam, he requested that we send him audio tapes of his favorite music and we did.

When Nick got together with his friends, they would act silly and joked around with me and made me laugh. Considering our turbulent childhood, those jokes made my life and Nick's bearable. Our mother was divorced and remarried many times, so Nick was more like a parent and taught me so many things. Our father left home and never returned when I was just 3 years old and Nick was 7. He never paid child support or visited us, not even on birthdays or Christmas. Needless to say, our childhood was not a happy childhood, but Nick managed to hold hope for the future. He reminded me that good days were ahead when we could get out and make our lives the way that we wanted them to be. I admired his wisdom and strength and especially his caring.

Nick enlisted in the Marine Corps in 1966. At the time of his enlistment, he was a freshman at the University of Cincinnati, majoring in Liberal Arts. At that time, the topic of the day was the war in Vietnam. The daily headlines in the local newspapers and the 6 o'clock news was about the Communist North Vietnam's attempt at invading South Vietnam and taking control. Nick felt bad for the South Vietnamese people. He enlisted to help stop the spread of Communism and he truly believed that he and his fellow Marines were helping. He also believed that protecting their freedom was as important as protecting the freedom of United States citizens.

*The tour of duty for the troops in Vietnam was 13 months. I remember getting a letter from Nick which said, **"This is the last letter you will get from me. The next time that I see you will be in person. I*** *have served my 13 months. I am scheduled to go to Okinawa for two weeks of R&R (rest and relaxation) and then I will be home."*

In early September, 1967, I was a sixteen year old high school student. That first weekend of September, my Uncle Joe and I went to the Pony Keg (a store that sold beverages and snacks). We were preparing for a Labor Day party. When my Uncle Joe and I returned, we saw a strange car in the driveway. It was an olive drab color with yellow letters stenciled on the side, "U.S.M.C." Acting very nervous, my uncle turned the car around and said he had forgotten something at the store. I knew he wasn't telling the truth. I saw the car. I thought to myself, *"He's home! My dearly loved brother is home! They are having a surprise for me!"* So I played along with my nervous uncle and returned to the store with him, all along inside I was screaming with joy. My brother was my only true family and he was finally home. I couldn't wait to hug him tight. When Uncle Joe finally took me back home, the Marine Corps sedan was gone. I ran into the house with joy as high as a kite. To this day, I have never gone from the highest high to the lowest low within seconds like I did then. The Marines had come to our house to deliver the devastating news that Nick had been killed.

It took two weeks for Nick's body to come home. I had to go to the Catherman and Jones Funeral Home to identify Nick's body. Ironically, that was the same place Nick took me as a child to trick or treat on Halloween because they gave out rainbow lollipops the size of saucers. My memories of Nick came flooding in.

The following year I received a letter from a Marine by the name of David who had just met Nick before Nick was killed. David had just arrived in Vietnam on the 2nd of September. He said that Nick was very kind to him and showed him around the battery. That evening, Nick was on duty as the Sergeant-of-the Guard. That's when the Viet Cong infiltrated the battery with mortar fire and satchel charges. Along with Nick, two other Marines died and three were wounded during the attack. David had talked to Nick just five minutes before the attack. He assured me that Nick did not suffer that night. David helped carry Nick to the med-evac helicopter after the attack died down. He said that when he first saw Nick's body, it appeared he was sleeping. He had a look of complete peace about him.

Was Nick a hero? To me he was, always. After he died, I was notified that he had taken out a small insurance policy and I was named his beneficiary. With that money I bought myself a used car. That was my freedom. Nick gave me the ticket to start my own life. I no longer felt trapped.

I miss him terribly still. I only wish that my two grown sons could have known their Uncle Nick. Sometimes I can feel Nick's amazing spirit, like right now as I tell you this story. My throat tightens with sadness, but also with deep, deep gratitude. I feel so lucky and blessed to have had him for the years that I did. No girl could have had a better brother.

Please say hello to him for me when you visit the Wall Jennifer. I have never been there. Someday, I plan to go. Not only do I grieve the loss of my brother, but also the more than 58,000 men that paid the ultimate sacrifice while trying to stop an evil communist force from taking over the helpless people of South Vietnam.

You will stand before the Wall and maybe feel the loss and love that must be soaked into the stone and earth by now. I will think of you on that day. Have a good trip and thank you for asking about my brother Nick.

Fondly,
Samantha (Cindy Wagman)

The Fourth Battalion, Eleventh Marines Command Chronology for September 1967 reports that a provisional Battery N was established to provide artillery for the First Marine Division's counter-rocket-fire plan. Battery N was emplaced along Highway 545 at the northern foot of Hill 306, about ten kilometers west of Da Nang.

Corporal Wagman's squad was providing security for Battery N on the morning of September 2, 1967. At about 12:15 a.m., while Cpl. Wagman was checking his sentries on post, his position was suddenly attacked by an enemy force of undetermined size. Cpl. Wagman and two other Marines were killed by shrapnel from explosive charges thrown by the enemy in the ensuing fight.

Nicholas Owen Wagman's name is located on the Vietnam Memorial Wall, panel 25E, line 090.

Our Defenders

Oh, look out upon the green fields.
What a glorious sight to behold.
Here buried one next to another,
Our defenders, the young and the old.

How proudly each stone stands before us
And each flag waves on the breeze.
How gallantly each gave a life
So others could rest safe at ease.

Oh, see there the brown earth among them;
The flowers and wreaths still so grand.
Another defender of freedom
Lies still now, with honor in hand.

Go rest our defender, so weary.
You've done your job bravely and true.
Know others stand now at the ready
To fight for the Red, White, and Blue.

Caroline Ann Silk

TERRENCE RAYMOND ROACH JR.

The Class of '67 is a book self-published by retired Marine Lieutenant Colonel Jack Wells. The book was given to me by my friend, retired Marine M.Sgt. Lawrence (Pete) Peterson. Pete served briefly with Mr. Wells in Vietnam in 1968. They met some thirty years later at a reunion and reestablished a friendship. Pete gave me Mr. Well's phone number, and after my phone conversation with Mr. Wells, the tight-knit camaraderie of the Marine Corps has, again, strengthened.

The Sixth Basic Class of 1967 (BC 67) convened on June 7, 1967, and graduated 498 second lieutenants on November 1, 1967. BC 67 sent more lieutenants off to war and suffered more officers killed or wounded than any basic school class since the Korean War.

In *The Class of '67'*, Jack Wells tells the stories of those classmates that gave everything. One of those classmates was Second Lieutenant Terrence R. Roach Jr. I would like to thank Mr. Wells for allowing me to use his chapter of Second Lieutenant Roach in my book.

Terrence Raymond Roach Jr. grew up in Birmingham, Michigan, with two sisters. His mother and father were in Vaudeville and were passionate about their Irish heritage and Christian beliefs. Friends recall that it was uplifting, positive, and a joy to be around the Roach family as well as entertaining.

Confident and free spirited throughout high school, Terry was once suspended for wearing a kilt to class. During high school, he played on the varsity baseball team. After graduating from Seaholm High School in 1960, Terry and his friend Tony Martinaitis were going to join the Army. Terry changed his mind and decided to enlist in the Marine Corps Reserve. Following recruit training in Parris Island, South Carolina, and six months of active duty, Terry returned home and enrolled at Wayne State University in Detroit. Tony Martinaitis recalls, "Terry enlisted in the Marines. The Marines! Terry wanted more than anything to be a Jarhead. Oh God, how I miss him."

Terry Roach loved Irish history almost as much as he loved Irish music. He met his future wife, Lynn O'Connor, at the Irish Music Club at Wayne State. Proud of his Irish background, Terry loved to sing Irish fight songs in the student union. At Wayne State, he was famous for wearing his Irish kilts to class ... and without getting suspended.

In Terry's sophomore year, he applied for the Platoon Leaders Class (PLC) program offered by the United States Marine Corps, which led to a commission as a second lieutenant upon graduation from college. In the summer of 1966, Terry attended the ten-week PLC training at Quantico, Virginia. He successfully completed the course in August and returned to Wayne State where he graduated that following December.

In May 1967, Terrence R. Roach Jr. and Lynn O'Connor were married. In June, after a short honeymoon, they went to Quantico where Terry would begin Basic Class 6-67.

The student platoon assignments were arranged alphabetically. Terry was overjoyed to see an old friend, Tom Rainey, whom he knew from PLC.

On a crisp fall day on November 1, Basic Class 6-67 graduated at a ceremony in the Marine Corps School Theater in Quantico. Terry and most of the 498 freshly commissioned second lieutenants immediately received orders for Vietnam.

Terry had a month to get his affairs in order. He took Lynn back to Michigan and got her settled into a new home and spent the rest of his leave enjoying his time with his new wife.

On November 30, Terry flew to Norton Air Force Base in California where he met a group of his former classmates. After shaking hands and getting caught up, the new lieutenants boarded their flight to Southeast Asia. There was a two-day layover in Okinawa before arriving at Da Nang on December 2.

Terry and those with Third Marine Division orders flew by C-130 to Phu Bai where they were briefed on the enemy situation by the commanding general. Terry wanted more than anything to get command of a rifle platoon. To increase his chances, he hitched a ride on a truck convoy going to Camp Evans to report ahead of the other lieutenants.

His strategy paid off. Upon his arrival at Camp Evans, located just thirteen miles northwest of Hue City in the I Corp, Second Lieutenant Terrence Roach Jr. was assigned to First Platoon, Alpha Company, First Battalion, Ninth Marines (1/9). The routine for the platoons of Alpha Company were day and night patrols, ambushes, and listening posts in the area around Camp Evans and along Highway 1. During the Indochina War, the French called this section of Highway 1 in the Quang Tri Province "The Street Without Joy."

In the latter part of December, Terry's platoon had several skirmishes with the Viet Cong and NVA, during which his platoon sergeant and a corpsman were killed.

Farther north of Camp Evans, around Khe Sanh, the final weeks of December till January 1968 were deceivingly quiet, even as hundreds of North Vietnamese soldiers poured into the surrounding hills and valleys. This lull changed after midnight on January 20, when North Vietnamese forces launched an attack on Hill 861. Early in the attack, the command bunker took a direct hit by enemy mortar fire, severely wounding the company commander and the first sergeant. The Tet Offensive of 1968 was now in effect.

One month after arriving in Vietnam, Terry's classmate, First Lieutenant Jerry Saulsbury, assumed command of Kilo Company, Third Battalion, Twenty-Sixth Marines. Early that same morning, an NVA artillery barrage struck the Khe Sanh Combat base. A direct hit on an ammunition supply point detonated 1,500 tons of ammunition. Destruction was widespread throughout the base from the barrage and the exploding ammo dump.

Two days later on January 22, the 1/9 Marines were ordered to move from Camp Evans to reinforce Khe Sanh. The battalion became under operational control of the Twenty-Sixth Marine Regiment, headquartered at Khe Sanh.

The next day, First Platoon, reinforced by Weapons Platoon, went to a small hill referred to as Alpha 1, in reference to First Platoon, Alpha Company. The position was also called Hill 64, referring to the number of Marines on the hill, unlike other hills in the country that were designated by the number of meters in height. This was done to mislead NVA that monitored Marine radio transmissions. Located about 500 meters in front of the 1/9 command position at the Rock Quarry, the Marines on Hill 64 were forward security for the battalion and were to provide early warning for attacks against the Khe Sanh Combat Base.

Nights were always terrifying on Hill 64 as heavy fog rolled in around sunset and would not lift until after dawn. The nights always seemed filled with sounds of things moving around the northwest side of the hill, and the Marines strained to see in the fog and the darkness. Tension was high on Hill 64 after division intelligence reported that electronic sensors detected another North Vietnamese Army regiment moving into the area.

Terry did everything he could think of to prepare his men and the Hill 64 defenses for the expected attack by the NVA. He instructed his squad leaders that in the event of an attack, the Marines were to stay out of the bunkers to avoid being trapped if NVA soldiers got inside the defensive wire. Terry had his corpsmen go to each bunker to give refresher training on basic combat first aid. The Navy chaplain for the battalion, Lieutenant Jack Heino, went out to the Hill 64 outpost and held religious services for the men.

In one of Terry's letters to Lynn, he wrote about his platoon radio operator, Lance Corporal Jim Rizzo. Terry wrote:

> *I put Rizzo up for a Bronze Star medal for his actions during Operation Badger Tooth. He is a fine young Marine. Men like Rizzo really make me feel proud of our country and the Marine Corps. Rizzo is going home in April and will go to Kent State University after he gets out of the Marine Corps.*

The bonds between a platoon commander and his radio operator were strong. Twenty-four hours a day, they were never far from each other and shared the same bunker. The platoon radio had to be monitored day and night. Platoon commanders and their radio operators were among the primary targets in any attack by NVA and Viet Cong.

Around 0300 on February 5, Terry's men could hear the attack by two hundred NVA sappers that breached Echo Company's Second Battalion, Twenty-Sixth Marines defensive wire on Hill 861A, two miles to the north. Classmates 2nd Lts. Jeff Bodenweiser and Don Shanley and their men were fighting for their lives.

Two days later, hundreds of North Vietnamese soldiers, supported by tanks, attacked and overran the Lang Vei Special Forces Camp near the Laos border. It was the first time enemy tanks had been used against Americans since the Korean War.

On a daily basis, Terry checked the defensive positions on the hill and verified the artillery and mortar defensive fires with a forward observer from Delta Battery, Private First Class Larry Seavy-Cioffi, who had arrived on Hill 64 three days earlier. Larry remembers Lieutenant Roach as an intense officer who seemed preoccupied with the responsibility that he bore for the men on the hill. In a philosophical discussion over C-ration coffee one morning, Larry remembers Lt. Roach saying, "God is my rock," when talking about the imminent threat the Marines were facing. Terry wanted to send out patrols forward of the hill, but the request was denied by the battalion commander because it was considered too dangerous.

Around 0100 on February 8, there seemed to be more movement than usual outside the tangle of concertina wire surrounding the hill. Around 0300, Terry moved around the hill, checking up on his Marines. A little after 0400, the hill erupted with a barrage of mortar fire from the NVA's 101D Regiment, forcing the Marines to take cover within their bunkers. The sound of a bugle signaled the attack.

Eighteen-year-old Private First Class Ed Welchel's bunker on the west side of Hill 64 was the first to get hit by chicom grenades and a red smoke grenade. The concussion from the grenades blew Welchel's helmet off, throwing him against the wall of the bunker and knocking his rifle out of his hands. Choking red smoke filled the bunker. Lt. Roach immediately rushed to the bunker and assisted the stunned Marine to the relative safety of another bunker. Lt. Roach then moved into the smoke and darkness to rally his Marines on the west side of Hill 64 against the attack.

Minutes later, the barrage ceased, and the attacking NVA threw canvas on top of the concertina wire and breached the Hill 64 defensive positions in two places. Terry quickly assembled a squad of his men and led them forward against the NVA who were now inside the defensive wire. While moving along a trench line toward the attacking enemy soldiers and firing his M-16 rifle, Lt. Terry Roach was killed.

Fifty-one Marines and Navy Corpsmen on Hill 64 were killed or wounded during the furious battle. At first light, a relief force from Second Platoon, led by the company commander, Captain Mac Radcliffe, drove the NVA attackers off the hill and relieved the gallant Marines on Hill 64 who battled the numerically superior NVA force with such a ferocity that they prevented the enemy from taking total control of the hill. After evacuation of the dead and wounded, Alpha Company was ordered to abandon the position, and air strikes were brought in to destroy any positions that might subsequently be used by communist forces.

Second Lieutenant Terrence R. Roach Jr. was awarded the Bronze Star Medal with Combat V posthumously for his heroic actions on Hill 64. An excerpt of the citation states:

> *For heroic achievement in connection with operations against the*
> *enemy in the Republic of Vietnam while serving as platoon commander*
> *with Company A, First Battalion, Ninth Marines, Third Marine*
> *Division. During the early morning hours on 8 February 1968, Second*
> *Lieutenant Roach's platoon was occupying an observation post*
> *northeast of Khe Sanh Combat Base. Suddenly, the Marines came under*
> *small arms and mortar fire supporting an aggressive ground assault*
> *by two North Vietnamese Army companies. Disregarding his own safety,*
> *Second Lieutenant Roach unhesitatingly left his covered position and*
> *fearlessly moved about the fire-swept terrain . . . he fearlessly*
> *engaged the enemy in hand-to-hand combat until he was mortally*
> *wounded. His heroic and timely actions inspired all who served with*
> *him and were instrumental in preventing his unit from being overrun.*
> *Second Lieutenant Roach's courage, superb leadership and selfless*
> *devotion to duty were in keeping with the highest traditions of the*
> *United States Naval service.*

Lynn and Terry's family were devastated when told of his death in Vietnam. On a cold winter day at Sacred Heart Cemetery in Detroit, Terry was buried with honors. Three months later, his daughter, Mary Scott, was born. Terry's father never recovered from the shock of Terry's death, and for the final years of his life, after brewing his traditional morning coffee, with a tear in his eye, would always make a toast to his son and the Corps.

At times, the company commander of Alpha 1/9, Captain Mac Radcliffe, finds himself waking up in the early-morning darkness hearing the voice of Lance Corporal Rizzo saying, "Skipper, they are all around us, you got to come and get us."

Terry's daughter is now married with a family of her own. Mary Scott named her son Terrence in honor and memory of the father that she never saw, taken from her in the battle on Hill 64.

Terrence Raymond Roach Jr.'s name is located on the Vietnam Memorial Wall, panel 38E, line 038.

Imagine

Imagine yourself in a place where you are at the peak of your life. A place where every moment means something.

Imagine yourself all alone there. Then imagine the best people you will ever meet in your life join you.

Now imagine that you know that each second could be your last. That each thought could be your last too. That any one of your friends could be dead at any moment.

If you can imagine all of this you can feel for an instant what it was like for those of us who served in Vietnam.

Sgt. John Spiizzirri
www.angelfire.com/ny2/SGTFATS/page1.html

SIGFRID R. KARLSTROM

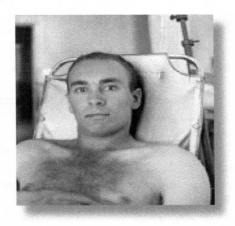

In May 2006, I visited my daughter who was living in Sumner, Washington, at the time. While there, I came across a *Seattle Times* newspaper, and inside was an article titled "A Life Lost in Vietnam: The Truth Comes Late," written by Alex Fryer. It was an interesting story about a Seattle native who died in Vietnam forty-three days after he was wounded. The photo above was taken after Sigfrid Karlstrom was wounded. He appears to be in pretty good condition. After reading the article, I went to the Virtual Wall website and found Lt. Karlstrom's memorial posted by many friends and his sister, Ingrid Karlstrom. Through e-mail, I contacted Ingrid and told her of my wishes to include her brother in this book. She was most gracious and quite honored for me to "keep the flame lit." Not just for her brother, but for all who made the ultimate sacrifice.

Thank you, Ingrid, and thank you, *Seattle Times* staff writer Alex Fryer, for their contribution to this chapter.

The ancient Greeks figured three goddesses of fate gave mortals their share of good and evil. How else could they explain life's randomness, the fact that you can roll the dice ten times and get sixes on every toss, or none at all?

On Memorial Day, as we remember those who have fallen in war, fate seems to wind through thousands of stories, determining who lived and who died.

For twenty-three-year-old Sigfrid Karlstrom, fate folded his dreams of becoming a diplomat and sent him to South Vietnam. And fate again intervened on an April day in 1967 when he crossed into a Montanyard village in the Central Highlands, into the guns of the waiting Viet Cong.

Karlstrom's commander, retired Major Richard "Pete" Jones, never told Karlstrom's family the details of his death, how their son's life may have hinged on a single telephone conversation. Now he tells the story with weariness in his voice, as if accepting that fate requires enormous strength.

When Jan Karlstrom, Sigfrid's younger brother, recently learned what exactly happened that day in Vietnam, he simply sighed and said, "I don't know if you can feel worse after nearly forty years. It's just another fact about something very bad."

Sigfrid Karlstrom, the eldest of four children, graduated from Chief Sealth High School in 1961. He sold shoes at Sears to earn money to attend the University of Washington. His uncle worked for the State Department, and Karlstrom aimed his life in the same direction, learning to speak fluent Spanish, Russian, German, and Czech.

To help pay for college and increase his chances of becoming a diplomat, Karlstrom joined the Reserve Officers Training Corps, or ROTC, which sent him into the Army after graduation.

Nobody thought much about Vietnam at the time. But that changed in 1964, after North Vietnamese gunboats allegedly attacked two US destroyers in the Gulf of Tonkin and President Lyndon Johnson vowed to send more troops.

The ROTC, which had promised Karlstrom entry into the Foreign Service, suddenly channeled him into an unexpected direction.

Karlstrom was assigned to a six-member civil-affairs team led by Jones, a captain in 1967. Lightly armed, team members aimed to win over hearts and minds of Vietnamese villagers near the Cambodian border by providing medical care and teaching new ways to grow rice.

Captain Jones had a rule: None of his men would enter the same village on successive days. The enemy watched for patterns and would try to ambush returning American soldiers, he reasoned.

In mid-April, Captain Jones took a couple of days of R & R to pick up the unit's paychecks in Nha Trang, not far from Saigon. While he was traveling, he called Karlstrom, who told him that another captain had ordered him back into a village he had just visited. When Karlstrom argued that it was against team policy, the captain pulled rank and ordered him to return to the village. Jones was adamant. He told Karlstrom, "Don't go. Disobey the order."

But through all these years, Jones has never been certain whether Karlstrom actually heard him. The telephone lines across South Vietnam were notoriously unreliable.

When Captain Jones returned to the unit, he learned that Karlstrom had led a group of men to the village, and they were attacked by an unknown number of Viet Cong while crossing a gulley. A bullet pierced Karlstrom's hip, and he was evacuated to a hospital at Clark Air Force Base in the Philippines. Karlstrom was the only team member wounded.

A few weeks later, Karlstrom wrote a letter to his anxious parents.

> *Dear patient waiters, I was sent to Clark Air Force Base where something went wrong and I had further surgery. Since then, I have been subjected to the dubious pleasure of recuperation. The bullet entered the left leg near the joint, fracturing the pelvis. It messed up the rectal colon somewhat so now I have a colostomy which will be rehooked up later. I have a 3X6 open wound on the left thigh which will require skin grafts. Getting tired now, so will close. I appreciate your letters and will try to reciprocate better. Say hello for me, Sig.*

Jan Karlstrom still has the yellow telegrams from the secretary of the Army. The first tells his parents that their son had been "slightly wounded." The others say his wounds were dire but survivable. The seventh telegram, received after a chaplain visited his West Seattle home, regrets to report that Karlstrom died on May 26, 1967. Jan was a teenager at the time.

Over the years, Karlstrom's parents came to quietly oppose the Vietnam War, but they were more saddened than strident.

As for the details of his brother's death, Jan said he heard there was some kind of problem but never knew the details. "I always had the impression that Sigfrid felt responsible, that it was somehow his decision to go back. I hadn't heard that he was ordered back against policy," said Jan, adding, "There's so many things like that."

In the days after Karlstrom's death, Jones was so angry that he tracked down the captain who gave the order to return to the village and punched him in the face. "I knocked his ass over a bunch of sandbags," he said.

Jones never called Karlstrom's parents to tell them about the conflicting orders. He had heard that they were angry at the military and wouldn't be receptive to hearing from him. Jones offered his phone number in case Jan wanted to talk about his brother's death. Jan said he probably won't take up the offer. "Obviously, I'm not going to blame him, and figuring out who the other captain is makes as much sense as tracking down the guy who shot my brother."

Ingrid Karlstrom did not dwell on the hows and whys of her brother's death. The pain from such a devastating loss was tremendous, and the only way she could ease the pain was to remember the good times she shared with her brother during her childhood.

Sig was three and a half years older than I. Bernie came one year later, and then Jan was born three years after Bernie. So Sigfrid was a bit older than us and was the typical "big brother."

Sigfrid could be the bully at times and often ordered us around when he wasn't hanging out with his friends. Even with Sigfrid pulling rank on us, he was also very protective. When I was in first grade at Fauntleroy Grade School, I was walking home by myself after school, and a couple of older boys got in my way and started bullying me. Very fortunate for me, Sigfrid came along and saved the day. He got in their face and told them to pick on someone their own size. I think he was inviting the bullies to pick on him. They ran away, and Sigfrid walked me the rest of the way home. I'm sure that I didn't know the meaning of the word pride, *but I am sure that is what I felt when Sigfrid came to my rescue.*

I remember one time while the family was at the dinner table, and Sigfrid was about thirteen years old. Everyone called him Siggie up until then. Dad made the announcement that we would all be calling him Sigfrid from then on. Sigfrid was growing up and was acting more like an adult. However, he kind of blew that image when he decided to tell a joke about a guy who ate too many beans and could be seen lifting one of his cheeks off his chair every so often, which Sigfrid demonstrated.

I often think of Sigfrid, good but sad thoughts. I think back often of our family growing up on that wonderful beach in West Seattle and the great times we had. At the time, I thought Sigfrid was bullying us, but now I believe he was just keeping us in line. That war in Vietnam deprived us and the world of Sigfrid's great talents and potential. He is missed by all who knew him.

Wulf Lindenau is currently the commander general of Military Order of Foreign Wars (MOFW). In 1965, He and Sigfrid Karlstrom served together as second lieutenants in the Army. While attending a civil affairs course in Fort Gordon, Georgia, they became very good friends.

Mr. Lindenau has fond memories of Sigfrid.

I first met Sig while serving with the 178th Intelligence Group in 1965. He spoke German and so did I. As a matter of fact, Sig spoke several languages. He also had a strong desire to become a foreign service officer with the US Department of State. We both had the same interests. I loved Sig like a brother. I was honored to have him stand with me as best man at my wedding.

Sigfrid was self-disciplined, motivated, had sound judgment, and the fortitude to be successful in any endeavor. I know he would have been a credit to the State Department.

Sigfrid was also an excellent tennis player. Many believed that he had the talent to be a professional tennis player. I believe he was the tennis champion of the First Army in 1965.

I often think of Sigfrid and the friendship that we had. I miss him dearly.

Sigfrid Karlstrom should not have gone back to that village. He should not have been wounded on that particular day in April 1967.

Sigfrid Karlstrom should not have died while hospitalized at Clark Air Force Base forty-three days later. The cause of death was from an infection. People should not die while hospitalized from infection. Irregardless of fate, Sigfrid Karlstrom's death was not in vain. He lived the life of a hero, and he died a hero. He will be missed but never forgotten.

Sigfrid R. Karlstrom's name is located on the Vietnam Memorial Wall, panel 20E, line 118.

Freedom is never more than one generation away from extinction. We didn't pass it to our children in the bloodstream. It must be fought for, protected, and handed on for them to do the same, or one day we will spend our sunset years telling our children and our children's children what it was once like in the United States of America where men were free.

—Ronald Reagan

INDEX

K

L

M

N

CPSIA information can be obtained
at www.ICGtesting.com
Printed in the USA
LVHW100016131122
733003LV00005B/181